Do it The Lazy Way

alpha books

1. Take a breather. Curl up with a kitty. Bathe the room in candlelight to soften the night. Nothing makes a room more wonderful with less effort than the simple act of lighting a candle.

2. To support your Lazy Way attitude, keep the KISS word (keep it simple, stupid) in your heart and mind at all times.

3. The less work you put into arranging flowers, the better they like it. In other words, if you let flowers be what they naturally are, you'll save time and they'll look their best.

4. When you're setting a table for a dinner party, go casual. Everyone will be glad you did. Comfort and ease are the watchwords for contemporary life.

5. Fold away the technology (okay, take the cell phone) when you feel deprived of Mother Nature's decorative power. Pack up a getaway and move it on out. Keep it as simple as possible so it doesn't feel like work.

*One luxurious
bubble bath*

*Access to most comfortable
chair and favorite TV show*

*One half-hour massage
(will need to recruit spouse, child, friend)*

... ...e CD

cut

6. Don't surrender to clutter. Meet the challenge head on so you'll be able to sit back and relax in comfort and peace. One small step at a time will do it.

7. You can double the impact of whatever you place in front of a mirror— a bouquet of flowers, a view of the room, the light from a window.

8. Protect your upholstery fabrics with a fabric protector before stains happen. You can wait longer to fix up your furniture.

9. Lazy is just another word for quick-witted. Lazy-style decorating is just another phrase that means discriminating.

10. To showcase a small rug at the center of a seating group, lay it on a larger sisal rug. The borders of the sisal rug that show around the small rug act as a frame to bring the rug into proportion with the rest of the room.

COUPON

COUPON

COUPON

COUPON

cut

Redecorate Your Home

Redecorate Your Home

Rebecca Jerdee

Macmillan • USA

Macmillan Publishing books may be purchased for business or sales promotional use. For information please write: Special Markets Department, Macmillan Publishing USA, 1633 Broadway, New York, NY 10019.

International Standard Book Number: 0-02-863163-3
Library of Congress Catalog Card Number: 99-63424

00 99   8 7 6 5 4 3 2 1

Interpretation of the printing code: the rightmost number of the first series of numbers is the year of the book's printing; the rightmost number of the second series of numbers is the number of the book's printing. For example, a printing code of 99-1 shows that the first printing occurred in 1999.

Book Design: Madhouse Studios

Page creation by Carrie Allen and Heather Pope

Printed in the United States of America

You Don't Have to Feel Guilty Anymore!

IT'S O.K. TO DO IT *THE LAZY WAY*!

It seems every time we turn around, we're given more responsibility, more information to absorb, more places we need to go, and more numbers, dates, and names to remember. Both our bodies and our minds are already on overload. And we know what happens next—cleaning the house, balancing the checkbook, and cooking dinner get put off until "tomorrow" and eventually fall by the wayside.

So let's be frank—we're all starting to feel a bit guilty about the dirty laundry, stacks of ATM slips, and Chinese takeout. Just thinking about tackling those terrible tasks makes you exhausted, right? If only there were an easy, effortless way to get this stuff done! (And done right!)

There is—*The Lazy Way*! By providing the pain-free way to do something—including tons of shortcuts and time-saving tips, as well as lists of all the stuff you'll ever need to get it done efficiently—*The Lazy Way* series cuts through all of the time-wasting thought processes and laborious exercises. You'll discover the secrets of those who have figured out *The Lazy Way*. You'll get things done in half the time it takes the average person—and then you will sit back and smugly consider those poor suckers who haven't discovered *The Lazy Way* yet. With *The Lazy Way*, you'll learn how to put in minimal effort and get maximum results so you can devote your attention and energy to the pleasures in life!

v

THE LAZY WAY PROMISE

Everyone on *The Lazy Way* staff promises that, if you adopt *The Lazy Way* philosophy, you'll never break a sweat, you'll barely lift a finger, you won't put strain on your brain, and you'll have plenty of time to put up your feet. We guarantee you will find that these activities are no longer hardships, since you're doing them *The Lazy Way*. We also firmly support taking breaks and encourage rewarding yourself (we even offer our suggestions in each book!). With *The Lazy Way*, the only thing you'll be overwhelmed by is all of your newfound free time!

THE LAZY WAY SPECIAL FEATURES

Every book in our series features the following sidebars in the margins, all designed to save you time and aggravation down the road.

- **"Quick 'n' Painless"**—shortcuts that get the job done fast.
- **"You'll Thank Yourself Later"**—advice that saves time down the road.
- **"A Complete Waste of Time"**—warnings that spare countless headaches and squandered hours.
- **"If You're So Inclined"**—optional tips for moments of inspired added effort.
- **"The Lazy Way"**—rewards to make the task more pleasurable.

If you've either decided to give up altogether or have taken a strong interest in the subject, you'll find information on hiring outside help with "How to Get Someone Else to Do It" as well as further reading recommendations in "If You Really Want More, Read These." In addition, there's an only-what-you-need-to-know glossary of terms and product names ("If You Don't Know What It Means, Look Here") as well as "It's Time for Your Reward"—fun and relaxing ways to treat yourself for a job well done.

With *The Lazy Way* series, you'll find that getting the job done has never been so painless!

Series Editor
Amy Gordon

Managing Editor
Robert Shuman

Editorial Director
Gary Krebs

Development Editor
Doris Cross

Director of Creative Services
Michele Laseau

Production Editor
Donna Wright

Cover Designer
Michael Freeland

What's in This Book

Decorating Is Like Dancing

You can approach decorating seriously (with study), or you can take it lightly, using your natural instincts to freewheel around your rooms. You're probably a light-spirited soul who would rather dance the two-step than learn ballet, and you have opened this book in the hope of finding the easy way out of redecorating your home.

You love the audacious concept—the idea of *The Lazy Way*, especially when applied to decorating. Your ears perked up when you first heard the words. "That's for me," you said. Then, you wanted more information, "What does lazy decorating look like? How can it happen for me?"

Here's the deal, sweetheart: You take on the 'tude (lazy attitude), I'll show you a few simple steps, and before you know it, you'll be a whirling dervish of the redecorating kind. You'll learn ways to ease into decorating that will give you the style and comfort you crave and the fun you deserve.

It's a *Lazy Way* promise.

This book is not about taking on the big challenge and winning the decorating contest. It's about breaking down what could be a daunting subject and managing it a few steps at a time. Although it includes every element of decorating, it doesn't imply that you must accomplish everything. Ever. The purpose of *Redecorate Your Home The Lazy Way* is to cover all the decorating bases so that you have a ready reference for whatever lazy decorating dance you want to learn.

Here's the first step to practice: Carve *The Lazy Way* mantra on your heart. It's just five, sweet words—"a little at a time, a little at a time."

The next step? Go to the back of this book; that's where you'll find the good stuff. The fun stuff. I always read a book from the back first. I figure that if it's still looking good at the end, it'll be worth its price tag. The back of this book is full of small-step, finishing-touch ideas you might want to try first. It's sort of like having dessert before eating your mashed potatoes, but hey, who's looking?

When you're ready to take a look at the entire contents of the book, you'll find it organized from the ground up: From solid walls, floors, and windows that need redecorating, to furniture and large accessories, to the final finishing touches of flower arranging, lighting candles, and throwing a beautiful party.

Part 1

Getting Your *Lazy Way* Attitude

Are You Too Lazy to Read "Getting Your *Lazy Way* Attitude?"

1 You think a color scheme is a new con game. ☐ yes ☐ no

2 When you set the table, it looks like it belongs in a flea market. ☐ yes ☐ no

3 You think a hardware store is somewhere you buy computers. ☐ yes ☐ no

one

Know the Carefree Decorator in Yourself

This'll put air in your tires: The decorating police have been picked up, charged with contempt, and put behind bars. They won't be hassling you about your decorating again. You can come out now and admit that you haven't had time to get it done, that you've been too busy with everything else— such as living.

You've had enough on your mind without having to think about decorating. So you didn't. It's just that even though your life is more than full, the nagging little voice in your decorating head is getting louder by the day. You don't want to live in a place that looks as if no one cares. You *do* care. And you don't want to hire someone to do your decorating for you. You want to do it yourself. Here's how:

- Painlessly
- Effortlessly
- Easily

A COMPLETE WASTE OF TIME

The 3 Worst Things to Do When Going *The Lazy Way:*

1. Pressure yourself to get things done.

2. Try to do everything all at once.

3. Beat yourself up when you don't.

YOU'RE IN GOOD COMPANY

In case you thought you were the only one hassled by decorating police, think again. There are a lot of decorating deadbeats out here, hiding behind closed doors that we wouldn't open to the critics.

But, hey, the jury's still out. Who says you can't manage a little decorating on the side—if it were short-circuited, cut down, and mapped out?

You've got it. It's called redecorating your home *The Lazy Way*. You won't have to go to school to learn how to do it. In fact, you already know a lot about decorating whether you realize it or not. It's just a matter of uncovering a few facts about your decorating persona, taking a leap into the world of lazy, and riding along with it.

WHAT'S YOUR DECORATING SIGN?

Okay, it's a stretch for a conversation opener, but humor me. If I asked you what your signature color is, what would you say? Are you aware of an inborn color habit or range of color choices you've carried with you much of your life? Could you put a name on your natural style or characteristic appearance? Are you traditional or modern in your thinking? Elegant, fussy, plain, trendy, or casual?

The answers to these questions and other fascinating truths are already in your possession. In this chapter, I walk you through practical ways to uncover your decorating sensibilities and clarify your personal style. This key information will give you the confidence to get started decorating *The Lazy Way*.

COLORS THAT CALL YOUR NAME

They're out there waiting. Hanging on racks in department stores. Soliciting in strip-mall shops. Begging for your attention in paint store displays and home centers. Hoping you'll come by to claim them.

Finding your color style might require a scavenger hunt of sorts:

- Look in your closet. See the skeletons? Your closet tells stories about your personal nature. It also expresses the way you created and keep your home. Select your favorite shirt, suit, blouse, or dress—the one that puts high self-esteem on your body. What color is it?

- Select another item of clothing that looks good on you and brings out your best skin tones. Note the color. Place the first two items of clothing together front-and-center on the closet pole.

- Select a third feel-good item to tuck in with the first two. Did you select colors in common, or are they all different?

Go shopping. If you could have anything you wanted from your favorite clothing store (disregard prices because you're not buying today), what colors would they be?

- Go to your usual clothing store and select three items of clothing whose colors appeal to you. Make a mental note of the colors.

- Repeat this step in an unfamiliar clothing store to see which colors trip your trigger. Do you notice a

QUICK ⊙ PAINLESS

Invite a friend on your color-and-style hunt. Friends often see your habits more clearly than you do.

repeated color choice that leads you toward your signature color, or are you coming up with a schizoid group of colors that leads to nothing but confusion?

If you're feeling confused, don't worry. You're just gathering clues. The next stop will reveal your signature color.

- Stop at a paint store. This isn't a test, and there are no wrong answers. A paint store stop will give you information to take home. It's also the first step in beginning your decorating diary or file.

- For a few quiet moments, stand in front of the interiors paint chip rack and clear your mind of all past paint and decorating experiences. Disconnect yourself from any fashion or clothing color experiences. Just let your hand go where your heart leads it. Choose the color that stands for you. This is your signature color.

- From the display, choose a second color that works with your signature color. Then, pick a third. Tell the paint-store clerk you'll be back.

Check out a home center. This stop might seem redundant when you already have your signature color in hand. However, one more crack at color chips would add nuances to your decorating file and underscore your color habits:

- Explore warm and cool variations of your signature color, collecting a few more paint chips for your

A COMPLETE WASTE OF TIME

The 3 Worst Things to Do When Making Your Style Search:

1. Hurry through it.

2. Make thoughtless selections.

3. Take a shortcut.

color box. Do you find yourself liking grayer, yellow, red, or blue versions?

- Investigate the tile section to see what you can add to your collection. (You might need to make a small tile purchase.) Find your signature color in the kitchen countertop section. Sometimes, laminate samples are available to take home. Make a signature selection from a variety of wood finish samples. Are you a light wood personality or one who likes your wood dark?

YOUR STYLE FILES

We all do it: clip and save. We collect pictures of rooms that inspire us to make decorating changes. At least, they help us imagine that we'll get around to it some day. The problem is that we never organize the bits and pieces, the icons of our decorating dreams. They, like a diary or a journal, reveal a composite picture of our desires. From desire comes action. If you haven't even made the first step toward creating a picture of your decorating self, here are some things you can do to start:

- It's only paper: Tear pages from magazines that inspire you to do what you see in the pictures. Be discriminating so you'll avoid cluttering your decorating portrait with disparate ideas. Assemble them on scrapbook pages, in pocketed folders, or in a file.

- Support your habit: Don't apologize for collecting print images that you respond to. Tuck them into a book, a folder, or a file next to your magazine tear

Buy yourself a picture book today. It's your reward for paying attention to the finer things in life. Choose a book that best represents your personal decorating style. Then, go home and lose yourself in the pictures.

The Lazy Way

sheets. Printed images can come from anywhere—a wonderful matchbox from a restaurant, the image on a program cover, anything that speaks to you and says, "I am like you. I represent your decorating style."

- Break open your memory bank: Remember the rooms of your childhood that welcomed you home, and visualize those that compelled you to stay when you visited. On paper, list the furnishings and colors present in those rooms. They may be comfort symbols and clues to your style. If you have a natural affinity for family heritage furnishings, draw upon them as part of your style.

- Map out a decorating plan: Call it decorating in stages, and begin with good foundation pieces: a sofa, a concert grand, a pair of upholstered chairs. In words or pictures, envision how, over a period of months or years, you will make changes that will move you toward a completed scheme. Then, don't beat yourself up if you change your plans or don't go through with any of it at all. This is just an exercise to build up your style muscles.

GETTING WITH THE LAZY PROGRAM

My friend Peggy has lazy-style decorating down cold. Ring her doorbell and you're greeted with exuberance. Step inside her home and you're blinded by the warmth and mood that permeates the place. Beyond her figure

YOU'LL THANK YOURSELF LATER

Don't be intimidated by others who have different tastes from your own and look down their long noses at your choices. Their instincts and opinions are theirs, not yours, and they get only one vote each.

in the doorway, your eye catches a glimpse of her deco-rating persona. A creaky, old wicker rocking chair eases up to a table graced with beaded lamplight and a flip-pant arrangement of backyard cuttings. In front of the fireplace, another table, winking with candlelight, holds the makings of an afternoon of fun. She could teach you a few things about relaxed decorating.

You settle into a comfortable old sectional, conve-nient side tables, and conversation. You feel good. But after a while, if you're a snoop like me, you wander away from the conversation to take a look around, getting her decorating details down in your cagey little mental note-book. Everywhere you look, you notice how a chair beck-ons you, books invite reading, and interesting objects wait to be examined. In every room, she has a place to live and be, eat and talk.

If you look past her charming arrangements of furni-ture and curious accessories, you begin to notice that the walls could use a little painting, and the edges of things seem singed by fireside smoke and burning candles. Near the ceilings, salvaged pieces hang existentially, appeas-ing the house's need for architectural interest without really building it in. When you visit her bedroom, she says, "I have to do something about this room! We've lived here seven years and I still don't know what to do with it. Maybe you could help me!"

Peggy makes you want to go home and redecorate—or, at least, pull a few of your favorite things out of hid-ing to arrange them in a place where you would appre-ciate them.

QUICK PAINLESS

Buy yourself a decorating diary with pockets for print images and color chips and blank sheets for making decorating plans. That way, everything is in one place. When the pock-ets bulge too much, go through them and thin them out; you'll see how your decorating whims have changed.

Here's how she'd tell you to do it:

- **Lazy Rule #1:** Avoid decorating on a tight schedule. Do it when the mood hits, the time feels right, or you feel a party coming on.

- **Lazy Rule #2:** Get out your personal favorites—collectible books, family pictures, hats, whatever—and decorate. Don't worry, the decorating police are still locked away, so you can try anything you like without fear of being caught in a decorating mistake.

- **Lazy Rule #3:** Play. Invite a friend over to help arrange your decorating toys. Practice small arrangements of collectibles, live with them a while, and then change them. Move furnishings from room to room, seeing what feels good, works better, and lives best.

- **Lazy Rule #4:** Think outside the box. Decorating rules are nice, but sometimes, they're boring and restricting, and your house just can't live up to all those standards.

- **Lazy Rule #5:** Follow your instincts. Develop eyes that see with your heart, and bring home new decorating toys only when they qualify as heartbreakers.

- **Lazy Rule #6:** Party. Special occasions are excuses for frivolous decorating and creating the impression that you're a decorating fool. You can fool a lot of people a lot of the time at a party. Everyone's so busy having a great time that they rarely see beyond the flowers you've arranged, the places you've set for them, or the food you serve.

IF YOU'RE SO
INCLINED

Scan your home for furniture, dishes, and accessories that qualify as lazy. Notice whether you're hoarding collections of stuff without putting them to use.

NAME THAT STYLE

Everyone has it—that elusive, inevitable way of presenting themselves to the world at large and to the world of work. It's a particular, distinctly characteristic way of acting, speaking, and writing. When it comes to living in a home and decorating it, style is distinctly yours in terms of how you spend money on it or display it.

What's your inherent style? If you're having trouble describing it or distinguishing it with a name, try this:

- On a piece of paper, list *your* colors, *your* style of furnishings, and *your* type of collectibles. Find a theme or common thread that binds them.

- Give your theme a name. When you do, you'll breathe life into your decorating personality, and from this point on, you'll feel more sure of who you are when you bring beauty and style to the life inside your home.

In case you're having trouble getting started at naming your own style, here's a list of decorating style names and what they look like:

- Coastal Cottage: A small, beach-white place on the water. You collect seashells and sailboats, folding deck chairs, tables, and blue-and-white picnic cloths. You sleep on driftwood decks and sail away to sleep in a rope hammock and a cloud-white comforter.

- Camp Style: A home patterned after a rustic cabin in the woods with fishing reels, wooden skis, antlers, canoe paddles, Adirondack furniture, birch-bark

YOU'LL THANK YOURSELF LATER

Is your decorating style still Early Parental Provincial? That's when you live with stuff you inherited from your parents. Of course, it's not your style, but the stuff is still worth something and it's handy for now. Make plans now for how you'll use it, abuse it, or lose it in the future.

frames, and wool blankets for living the outdoor life inside.

- Civilized Frontier: The wild, wild west of cowboy stuff—saddles, spurs, tin crosses, Navajo rugs, and woven blankets—gets tamed by Victorian bric-a-brac brought from the east coast.

- 50s Style: Palette-shaped coffee tables, molded plastic and plywood chairs, utility furniture, brightly colored pottery and glass, and a craze for houseplants will do it for you. Toss in shaggy, Scandinavian rya rugs in jewel-tones, abstract swirls, and geometric patterns, and you're over the top.

- Creative Salvage: Recycled scrap material and junk— old fireplace surrounds, cracked china, old wine bottles, crusty chandeliers, and old estate garden gates—give this radical chic style its starting-point accessories. After that, it's muslin and cheesecloth draperies and turning old things into furniture pieces they weren't meant to be.

- English Townhouse: A gloriously disheveled layering of floral-patterned Chintz draperies, needlepoint pillows, bell-pulls, and Oriental rugs that link the indoor furnishings to the flora and fauna of the English garden just outside the doors.

- Greek Island: Low, flat-topped houses with small shuttered windows provide a cool retreat from the sun. Blue-and-white fabric patterns, white-washed stucco, terra cotta pots, and tiled floors suggest that the living is easy on the vine-covered terrace.

IF YOU'RE SO INCLINED

Visit a decorating department in a library or bookstore to scan through decorating styles of the past and present. You might see some things you like.

House of the Rising Sun: Sheer simplicity and tranquility—sea-grass mats cover the floors, and shoji screens open to a miniature sand and rock landscaped garden. Cupboard doors glide back to reveal bedding and futons that will be spread on the floors to sleep on. You'll take tea from bone porcelain and eat simple meals with chopsticks.

Swedish Romantic: Airy, white-washed wood and stucco, unadorned windows that let in the sunlight, and high, narrow shelves lined with white china and crystal—all intended to reflect the lake water outside. Add a broad, generous dining table fitted with an Empire or Gustavian-style sofa and chairs and you sense the intended hospitality.

Farmhouse: Wholesome, corn-fed decorating that gives you the feeling of Grandma's house where she plied you with mashed potatoes and gravy, and you watched the fireflies flit about while you sat on the front-porch swing in the evening.

Simply Chic: The new minimalist look that's not as strict as it used to be. Now it's big and cushy, generous and spacious, and warmed by natural woods, rice paper shades, and greatly textured fabrics.

My Sister Shabby: The Paris apartment dweller collects flea-market fabrics, lamps, and cast-off furniture to layer together a sumptuous collection of velvets, silks, satins, feathers, ornamental ironwork, fancy finials, and filigrees.

YOU'LL THANK YOURSELF LATER

Collect all your mail-order catalogs in one place and toss out the old ones. Acquaint yourself with their contents to get an update on current styles.

THE LOOK OF LAZY

No matter what your personal style is, you can practice it in a *Lazy Way*. Every style has relaxed and easy elements.

The hallmarks of lazy are airy, uncluttered spaces lit by natural light and filled with generous, no-nonsense furnishings that invite relaxation and sitting-back comfort. It's simplicity without austerity, style without fuss. Colors are natural, fabrics care-free, and accessories straightforward and functional.

Natural Colors

To color rooms lazy, choose large amounts of warm, glowing whites—pale sunshine, paper moon, and white asparagus—for walls, curtains, bedspreads, and other large sections of color. For second colors to use in lesser amounts on table coverings, accent walls, or wall coverings, choose from pale sea, sky, and leaf tones. Pale taupes are good, too, because they add a sense of stone and earth. Reserve small amounts of hot-shot colors—the reds and oranges of fruit and flower—for energizing the rooms. The purposes of color in lazy rooms are gentility, serenity, and tranquility.

Lazy color names follow:

Pale Sunshine	Violet Rain
Quiet Refuge	Aegean Sky
Biscayne Bay	Water Bubble
Tide Pool	Ocean Spray
Corn Silk	Moon Slice
Sheer Apricot	Shell Flower

Rose Dawn	Strawberry Fields
Starlight	Serenity
Sea Breeze	Wading Pool
Effervescence	Silver Spring
Uphill	Wild Grass
Seedling	Mushroom

If I were to recommend warm-white background paint colors, I'd choose Pale Sunshine from Laura Ashley and Ivory Memento from Sherwin Williams. Dover White from Sherwin Williams is a good, basic white, too.

Easy-Care Fabrics

Lazy-style fabrics are the tried-and-true classics taken off the loom. Choose natural, washable, lightweight, and no-iron pieces. Lazy avoids the chaos of energetic, commanding fabric patterns and colors that come into a room to take it over. In the same way that you choose lazy colors, choose fabrics with a lot of airy, white backgrounds, open weaves, and simple patterning. Lazy loves taupe, green, and blue stripes and checks with an occasional dishtowel plaid tossed in. Another way to go is a singular floral or symbolic motif repeated on a light background with a lot of space between it and the next repeated motif. Here's a list of lazy fabrics:

100% cottons	Cotton canvas
Linens	T-shirt knits
Ticking	Chambray
Denims and twills	Flannels

Buy yourself a quart of your signature color for no reason. It's a symbol of your personal style to keep in your decorating closet.

The Lazy Way

Gather snippets of easy-care fabric swatches for your files as reminders of fabrics you'd like to incorporate into your decorating in the future. If you have no fabric sources, you can cut swatches from pictures in magazines and catalogs.

Brushed wool

Flour sacking

Sheer ivory voiles

Awning fabrics

Cotton chenille

Terrycloth

Cotton piques

Casual fabrics are everywhere, so your choices are never limited. The world at large is into easy-care, fuss-free fabrics, and manufacturers gladly oblige.

Sofa, So Good

It's back-to-basics comfort furniture if you're going *The Lazy Way*. Simple lines and shapes, generous cushioning, big backs, and seats covered in easy-care upholstery express this contemporary look.

Relaxed Dining

Large, generous ivory-white china, ironstone, and porcelain dishes and serving pieces are lazy tabletop icons. You'll choose hospitable, exaggerated sizes in soup and serving bowls and generous chargers to set under place settings. Simple patterns (if any at all) on dishes or cloths mean stripes, gentle swirls, huge checks, and a lot of open, white backgrounds.

Playing It Cool

Accessories such as rugs, lamps, vases, mirrors, and picture frames are plain rather than decorated, simple rather than complicated, and created from natural materials. Whether old junk or newly manufactured, accessories give lazy rooms their character. Popular materials? Galvanized metal, clear and beveled glass, light woods, enamelware, terra cotta, porcelain, natural wicker, and painted wrought iron.

When it comes to flowers, anything goes—except for fussy arrangements that take too much time to assemble.

LAZY-STYLE READING

Here's a list of books that, in different ways, relate to the philosophy of lazy redecorating. You'll find inspiration in each one of them:

- *The Art of Doing Nothing* by Veronique Vienne. Clarkson Potter/Publishers, New York, 1998.

- *Cut Flowers* by Tricia Guild. Clarkson Potter/Publishers, New York, *1998*.

- *Junk Style* by Melanie Molesworth. Stewart, Tabori and Chang, New York, 1998.

- *Pure Style* by Jane Cumberbatch. Stewart, Tabori and Chang, New York, 1998.

- *Summer* by Alice Gordon and Vincent Virga. Addison-Wesley Publishing Company, Inc., New York, 1990.

- *White by Design* by Bo Niles. Stewart, Tabori and Chang, New York, 1984.

Check Appendix B, "If You Really Want More, Read These" for other sources of inspiration.

Getting Time on Your Side

	The Old Way	The Lazy Way
Pulling your decorating act together	Years	2 weeks
Hiding from the decorating police	Years	You're out on bail
Envying the neighbors' perfectly decorated homes	Every time you go inside their house	Almost never
Asking friends for decorating advice	Too often	Almost never
Avoiding your mother-in-law's opinion about your decorating	Always	You can take it

Strain-Free Materials and Tools

Y ou'll love this: Stay right there in your easy chair while I run past a list of the most pain-free, convenient, and easy-to-use decorating materials and tools in America. I've explored the aisles of many home centers and decorating stores, checking them out for the latest shortcut opportunities you can buy right off the shelf.

Lazy Way decorating isn't a fan of every new invention on the market. In fact, its intention is totally discriminating. It aims to spot the quickest, shortest route to completing redecorating projects while getting them done well. Most *Lazy Way* materials and tools are familiar, tried-and-true products. A few are new, quicker-than-ever, easier-to-handle items that make yesterday's goods seem clumsy and out of sorts.

You might not be interested in all the redecorating projects outlined in this book. In fact, you're probably spot-checking it for a few, simple styling tricks or quick flower-arranging tips. For that reason, I've organized the second half

of this chapter into six specialty categories: Paint, wallpaper, window trimming, furniture care, picture hanging, and flower arranging. You can go right to your particular interest to find the tools and materials you'll need.

TOOLS FOR ALL REASONS

The list below contains basic, general-purpose tools.

- Can opener
- Carpenter's level
- Cellulose sponge
- Fabric shears
- Floral shears
- Hammer
- Long-nosed lighter
- Paper scissors
- Pliers
- Screwdrivers
- Stud sensor
- Tape measure
- Utility knife
- Window scraper
- Wire cutters
- Yardstick

If some of these items seem unfamiliar, you'll know them when you see them in the tool section of the hardware store or home improvement center. If you don't, ask for someone's help.

What Basic Tools Do

■ Can opener: You'll need one to open a paint can.

■ Carpenter's level: A measuring tool that comes with a "bubble" to let you know when the horizontal or vertical line you are measuring is on the level.

■ Cellulose sponge: A porous mass of absorbent plant material used to wipe up messes.

■ Fabric shears: Scissors made for and reserved for cutting fabric. Buy them in a fabric store.

■ Floral shears: Now, scissors for cutting flower stems come with notched blades to provide extra leverage when cutting stems and ribbon for floral bouquets. Some shears can be taken apart for easy cleaning by hand or in the dishwasher.

■ Hammer: Pounds nails. If it's a hammer with a claw, you can pull out nails. You'll need it for hanging mirrors and pictures.

■ Long-nosed lighter: A butane torch to light candles. Its long nose keeps fingers out of the way of fire.

■ Paper scissors: Scissors reserved for cutting paper.

■ Pliers: A slip-jointed tool for tightening eye screws in the backs of frames.

■ Screwdrivers: For turning screws. Buy two, a slotted screwdriver to turn screw heads with slots and a Phillips screwdriver to turn screw heads with crossed slots.

YOU'LL THANK YOURSELF LATER

While shopping for tools, handle the ones you plan to buy to be sure they feel comfortable in your hands.

- Stud sensor: This little plastic wonder has a magnet that locates metal fasteners in wall supports (studs) when you need the support for hanging pictures or fastening trims on walls. It will detect the presence of metal studs you'd also like to avoid. The stud finder puts a whole new spin on the old method of sleuthing for studs—tapping across a wall with a hammer, listening for the tight sounds where you hope a stud is standing.

- Tape measure: A plastic or metal palm-sized case with a pullout ruler. Good for measuring long lengths on walls, floors, windows, curtains, wall-covering borders, and rugs.

- Utility knife: A razor knife blade set at an angle for cutting cardboard and opening boxes.

- Window scraper: A single-edge razor holder for scraping paint and sticky labels off glass.

- Wire cutters: A clipper-like tool for cutting mirror- and picture-hanging wire.

- Yardstick: A sturdy, at-the-ready measuring tool for small lengths on windows, walls, and floors.

Home centers are trendy these days and so are powerful little gadgets. *Lazy Way* decorating doesn't require serious tools, but these are fun extras to consider.

Power Up the Basics

Once you put your hands on one of these electrical or battery-operated wonders, you'll be hooked. They take the pressure out of work, making it seem more like a power trip than a down-and-dirty job:

■ Cordless driver/drill/saw kit: A no-sweat, triple-duty luxury that comes with everything you need to drive screws, drill holes, and do general-purpose cutting. It will save elbow grease and muscle spasms and allow you to travel freely in a room without electrical cords. Just remember to recharge the battery, or you'll be turning the screws yourself.

■ Power staple gun and staples: Only worth renting if you have a number of dining room chair seats to upholster. It'll take the strain out of fastening the fabric to the bottoms of the seats.

■ Mouse sander: You'll fall in love with the electrical mouse sanding-and-polishing tool. It's shaped like a mouse or a tiny travel iron, is lightweight, and fits easily in the palm. Its sharp nose design gets into hard-to-reach flat areas, and an easy Velcro fastening system for replacing sandpaper pad tips speeds up your sanding and finishing work.

Put one of these tool teasers on your wish list so you can clear out the hand-powered tools in your toolbox. Just kidding. Nothing will ever replace good and simple tools.

SPECIAL TOOLS AND MATERIALS

A collection of basic tools gets you through general functions, such as hanging a mirror, attaching screws, and cutting decorating materials. For specific redecorating purposes, you'll need special tools and materials. On the next few pages, check the lists of stuff that will take you

YOU'LL THANK YOURSELF LATER

Ask to try demonstrator models in the tool section of a home-improvement center. It's free information you'll be glad to have.

through *The Lazy Way* of painting a wall, hanging a wall-paper border, hanging window treatments, taking care of your furniture, hanging pictures, and arranging flowers.

Easing Up Your Walls: Lazy Paint Tools and Materials

You can make painting a wall a breeze these days. Although there's not much new about painting with latex paint, the quality of the paint itself and the tools for getting it on the wall have improved.

Here's what you'll need for the least painful paint job on the planet:

- Bristle paintbrush
- Foam paintbrush
- Latex paint
- Nail hole filler
- Paint roller
- Painter's tape
- Painter's tray
- Roller extension handle

Look closely at the labels to be sure you're getting the materials and tools with the qualities described here:

- Bristle paintbrush: Buy a good quality synthetic-bristle brush to use with latex paint. Get one with the bristles cut at an angle.

- Foam paintbrush: An easy-going paint applicator made with rubber foam that's tapered at the end. It cleans up more easily than a bristle brush.

- Latex paint: Paint pigments suspended in a water base. It cleans up with water, unlike paints that are made with an oily base.

- Nail hole filler: Now, nail hole filler comes in a ready-to-use toothpaste-like tube with a convenient no-mess applicator at one end.

- Paint rollers: Buy an eight-inch-wide and a three-inch-wide synthetic-sleeved, non-splattering pair of rollers.

- Painter's tape: A low-tack masking tape used to mark off sections of the wall you don't want to touch with paint.

- Painter's tray: A wide, ribbed paint pan intended for use with a paint roller. It rests on an angle, giving you better paint distribution on the roller.

- Roller extension handle: A 30-inch wooden handle that screws into the end of a paint roller to make it possible to ease your high and low reaches.

Many paint stores also carry paper-hanging materials and tools. If your paint source is one you like, get them to help you with a simple border-hanging project.

Cutting Down the Paper Chase

Getting the goods for hanging a wallpaper border is easy. Manufacturers do their best to make wall decorating

QUICK ⬤ PAINLESS

Here's a tip from a painter about where to buy a non-splattering roller: Sherwin Williams.

effortless and fun for you. For example, these tempting products on the shelves are waiting to go home with you:

- Wall-covering borders
- Seam repair adhesive
- Wall-covering trim tools

In a specialty paint and paper store, you can get good help finding what you want. Here's what you can tell them you're looking for:

- Wall-covering borders: You're probably too young to remember gooey wallpaper paste and wall coverings with selvages you had to trim from the panel before hanging it on the wall. Pre-pasted wall coverings and borders are old news by now, but the newest news in borders is that they come with die-cut edges. They put exciting shapes on decorating borders and into room schemes.

- Seam repair adhesive: For stubborn wall-covering border seams that won't behave themselves, there are handy, pointed-tip tubes of stick-easy all-purpose glue.

- Wall-covering trim tool: A triangular-shaped combination trim tool that marks and cuts wall covering. Its retractable blade angles into corners.

In paint stores such as Sherwin Williams, you'll find not only the paints and wall coverings you want, but blinds and shades as well. They'll give you a leg up on

YOU'LL THANK YOURSELF LATER

Make use of the library check-out policy many wall-covering stores have for sample books. You'll be glad you took one home to look at papers in the environment where the one you're choosing will hang.

measuring for basic window coverings and custom-order them for you without charge. Home-improvement centers also offer the same services.

Cut-the-Hassle Window Trimmings

You can get basic blinds and shades from the decorating sections of home centers and paint stores, but home stores and super stores will also carry curtains and curtain-hanging hardware. Here's a basic shopping list:

- Blinds
- Curtains
- Decorative window hardware
- Magnetic rods
- Shades
- Tension rods
- Window hardware

Check the labels to be sure of what you're buying, especially when it comes to the measurements of curtain rods and fabric panels that will fit your windows when you get home:

- Blinds: Three-dimensional panels of paper, plastic, or metal that hang from brackets in windows and provide privacy.
- Curtains: Relaxed and simple-to-hang decorative fabric panels that soften the hard edges of blinds or shades. Look for simple curtains with tab-top hanging loops or the classic rod-pocked versions that slide over non-decorative tension rods.

QUICK ☻ PAINLESS

While you're waiting for a can of paint you ordered to be mixed, check out the other decorating tools and materials available in the paint store.

■ Decorative window hardware: A multitude of interchangeable curtain rods, brackets (for attaching the rods on the window frame) and finials (decorative embellishments to fasten on the ends of the rods), sold separately, allow you to mix and match until you get the window hardware look you love. You'll need a screwdriver to hang decorative curtain rods.

■ Magnetic rods: Would you believe magnetic curtain rods? No screws and tools needed. These 6- to 14-inch long rods, created for steel-surfaced doors and windows, thread through a curtain panel and snap themselves in place.

■ Shades: Flat privacy panels of paper, wood, or plastic that hang from hooks or brackets on window frames.

■ Tension rods: Curtain hangers that thread through curtain rod pockets and hang between the sides of the window frame by means of pressure released in springs inside the rod. No hardware is needed to hang tension rods.

Hardware stores and super stores with good hardware and housewares departments can supply you with more than curtain-hanging supplies. While you're shopping for curtains, pick up a few furniture care items in the same store.

Furniture Care

One thing leads to another. While you're picking up a can of fabric protector, you can pick up a few more furniture care items:

- Cheesecloth

- Fabric protector

- Tack cloth

- Tung oil

- Self-sticking protector pads

- Spot lifter

- Wood-finish stain marker

Read the fine print before you purchase to be sure these are the products you're buying:

- Cheesecloth: A loose, inexpensive, open-weave fabric used to apply an oil finish to wood furniture.

- Fabric protector: Repels water and spills without changing the look or feel of the fabric.

- Tack cloth: A cloth impregnated with a resin that attracts every last particle of dust and undesirable materials found on the surface you're about to refinish with Tung oil.

- Tung oil: A quick, natural oil wood finish you can put on with cheesecloth in just a few minutes. It creates a remarkably durable luster without all the fuss of other wood stains.

- Self-sticking protector pads: Felt or velour pads to put on the bottoms of lamps and accessories to protect tabletops from scratches.

YOU'LL THANK YOURSELF LATER

Floor protectors for the legs on your furniture pieces are good additions to your shopping list. Rubber coasters or felt pads will do the trick.

■ Spot lifter: A fabric stain remover in a can.

■ Wood-finish stain marker: Touch up scratches in your wood furniture with this ready-to-go color marker in a matching wood tone.

One-stop shopping is really the best (laziest) way to go. But you really have to pull your lists together. While you're in the super-store housewares department, slip through the frame department to pick up some ready-made frames. Also, check for any picture-hanging helps on the next list.

Perfect Picture Hanging

Get as many ready-to-hang picture frames as you can. Then, supply yourself with these products to do the projects in this book:

■ Frame kits

■ Magnetic tape

■ Picture-hanging kits

You'll find frame kits in specialty frame stores, not general home stores. Any hardware or home center will have the rest of what you need for hanging pictures.

■ Frame kits: Metallic frames come complete with pre-cut and ready-to-assemble parts and a key to turn the screws.

■ Magnetic tape: A roll of adhesive-backed, magnetized, flexible plastic tape that you can cut with scissors and stick on the backs of snapshots and small objects you'd like to attach to metal surfaces.

QUICK ■■ *PAINLESS*

Read the caution labels on containers to make sure you'll want to use them.

- Picture-hanging kits: Here's a convenient package that supplies you with wire, hooks, and nails. Buy them in hardware sections at discount and hardware stores.

A lot of what you buy depends on the pictures you want to display. Think of pictures as house jewelry, something you'll always be shopping for, collecting, and hanging.

Flower Arranging

Lazy flower arranging doesn't require much in the way of materials and tools. Flowers themselves supply most of your decorating material. All you'll need are some vases and these products:

- Floral clay
- Floral foam
- Decorative stones
- Marbles

If you don't know why you'd want these items, here's what they'll do for you:

- Floral clay: A sticky, green plastic material that attaches two layers together. It works to hold floral foam securely in a dry container.

- Floral foam: Sometimes known by its brand name, Oasis, this soft brick of green foam allows you to push flower stems into it and holds them securely in place. It is also highly water-absorbent and keeps your stems well-watered.

YOU'LL THANK YOURSELF LATER

Buy extra picture-hanging wire in a separate package if you plan to hang many pictures. A picture-hanging kit might not have enough.

- Decorative stones: Pretty river-washed rocks come in black, brown, green, and white to place in flower vases as weights that will anchor your stems. If you use them in glass vases, you can also enjoy their beauty.

- Marbles: Like decorative stones, marbles weight vases, hold flower stems in place, and look pretty through glass containers.

Don't let these lists daunt your decorating desires. If one-stop shopping is too much to organize or funds don't allow you to purchase everything all at once, don't pressure yourself. After all, decorating and shopping are some of the pleasures—not pains—of life.

Getting Time on Your Side

	The Old Way	The Lazy Way
Papering a wall	3 hours	1 hour
Finding a tool in a store	20 minutes	3 minutes
Selecting a wall covering	3 hours	30 minutes
Choosing flowers	20 minutes	5 minutes
Daring to try something new	Seldom	Often
Choosing a paint color	30 minutes	5 minutes

The Lazy Decorator's Shortcuts

Are You Too Lazy to Read "The Lazy Decorator's Shortcuts?"

1 The last time you lit a candle was during a storm emergency. ☐ yes ☐ no

2 Your idea of a decorating shortcut is to cross the job off your list. ☐ yes ☐ no

3 When you can't find the scissors, you buy another pair. ☐ yes ☐ no

The Expressly-Yours Decorating Closet

Your decorating closet probably belongs to the "virtual reality" club, the kind of storage that exists mostly in your mind. Slipped neatly onto imaginary shelves behind make-believe doors, your hypothetical collection of decorating tools and supplies waits for your call to redecorate.

Don't you wish. The reality is more like this: You get an urge to hang a picture (seems like a simple task), and you spend 20 minutes hunting down a hammer in the garage. When you'd like to touch up a handrail the kids have worn down to its original surface, you drive five miles to the paint store for a brush because your last one dried up in its tin-can container.

UPGRADE YOUR DECORATING DUMPING GROUND

If you can't remember whether you dumped the remains of your last decorating project in the basement, the garage, the tool shed, the cupboard under the sink, or the hall closet, it's

time for an upgrade—something concrete, more convenient, and expressly yours. Until you name the place or assign a location "Decorating Storage Only," you'll continue to waste time hunting down your tools and duplicating your decorating supplies when you can't find them.

Here are some possibilities for spots to collect your decorating tools and materials:

- The bottom section of a hall closet

- Open shelving in the basement

- An armoire with basket containers

- Behind a screen in a corner of a room

- Large trunk at the end of the bed

- Fishing tackle box

- Carpenter's tool chest

If none of these ideas for a decorating supply closet works for you, find one that does. The point is to Name That Place. Once your decorating tools have an address, they're likely to return home and you'll always know where they are. You'll be counting the time you saved not looking for tools and the money you saved not purchasing duplicates.

THE DECORATING CLOSET

Once you've designated the spot, clear away any materials that don't belong in it, and decide where you can locate the groups of supplies that follow on the next few pages. If you're lucky enough to have the ideal situation—a hall closet with walls, shelves, and a door—take the color splurge; paint the walls of your decorating closet with your signature color. Every time you open the door, your color style will come right back at you, giving your redecorating spirits a lift.

Here's what to gather without getting too crazy. First, pull together all the supplies that you already have in the house. Then, buy yourself more decorating tools as funds allow.

SACRED TOOLS

Put your mark on the tools that belong to you. Tell thieves and burglars at your house that this particular red-handled hammer, this dangerously hot, hot-glue gun, and this streamlined little screwdriver set are intended exclusively for *Lazy Way* decorating that you alone are qualified to do. Then, store your highly valued decorating materials and tools in the following files.

In the Toolbox

Whether it's an old-fashioned, country-style toolbox you picked up at an antiques store, a well-used fishing-tackle box you begged off your uncle, or a brand-new metal carpenter's toolbox purchased at a home center, you'll always have these tools within easy grasp:

- Electric drill/driver kit (substitute for manual drills and screwdrivers)
- Fabric shears
- Fine sandpaper
- Flat screwdriver

QUICK ⬤ PAINLESS

When your decorating supplies are few, store everything in a fishing-tackle box. Or take a look at the variety of new toolboxes you can find at home-improvement centers.

YOU'LL THANK YOURSELF LATER

See those holes on the handles of paintbrushes and paint rollers? Fasten hooks or nails on the edge of your paint-supply shelf and hang them up.

- Garden shears
- Hammer
- Paper scissors
- Pencil
- Phillips screwdriver
- Picture-hanging kits
- Pliers
- Power staple gun (optional—borrow one for a small project)
- Ruler
- Small eye screws
- Small nails
- Staples
- Tape measure
- Utility knife
- Wall-covering trim tool
- Window scraper
- Wire cutters

Another tool storage option is to hang your tools on a pegboard. It's not a bad idea because more often than not, a single decorating project doesn't require an entire tool chest of tools.

On the Paint and Wall-Covering Shelf

Keep your wall decorating tools separate from the tool-box supplies. A wall decorating project rarely requires tools other than those made specifically for painting or wallpapering:

- Cellulose sponge
- Clean rags
- Nine- and four-inch-wide, non-spatter, synthetic-sleeved paint rollers with handles that will accept an extension handle
- Paint tray
- Painter's tape
- Plastic drop cloth
- A 30-inch roller extension handle
- Roller extension handle
- Stir-sticks
- Two-inch-wide, angled, synthetic-bristle paintbrush
- Wall-covering trim tools
- Water bucket

An optional tool to include in your painting supplies is a foam brush or two. They're inexpensive substitutes for bristle paintbrushes, easy to use, and easy to clean.

On the Wall

You might not have space in your decorating supply closet to hold large items. Just make mental notes of where the tools are located elsewhere in your house:

- Kitchen step stool
- Metal yardstick

QUICK ☉ PAINLESS

Mark your tools with your name. Use lettering on adhesive-backed paper, such as peel-and-stick kitchen labels or name tags sold in party stores.

When you need to measure windows or walls, you won't waste time looking for them. I hang my yardstick in my broom closet. It has a designated nail, which means it's always returned.

In a Styling Kit

During my stint as a stylist for a television home show, I worked with another stylist who showed up with this clever storage device: A fanny pack with everything she needed kept her tool-supplied and on the move around the set. She never had to retrace her steps to get the tools she needed.

You might not need a fanny pack to hold the supplies below. A small box will do, but think of this collection as your set of fine-tuning tools. They're intended for finishing touches and they are miniature in size:

- Can opener
- Craft knife
- Lighter
- Magnetic tape
- Miniature level
- Miniature screwdriver
- Miniature window scraper
- Needle-nose pliers
- Plumb bob
- Small scissors
- Cloth tape measure
- Travel sewing kit

YOU'LL THANK YOURSELF LATER

When you purchase a miniature tape measure for your styling kit, purchase a second one to carry in your backpack, purse, or pocket for shopping.

The Restoration Hardware catalog has gift sets of small tools and toolboxes that beg to be used. My favorite item is the 12-tools-in-your-pocket tool. It holds a needle-nose pliers, wire cutter, two knife blades, three screwdriver heads, ruler, file, cap and bottle openers, and a mini-saw.

On a Flower-Arranging Shelf

Ten-minute flower arranging is possible only if you don't have to spend ten minutes looking for your supplies. Keep it all together on a shelf, and you won't spend more than a few seconds choosing what you need from your "prop" closet:

- Floral foam blocks
- Tall, plastic flower bucket
- Garden shears
- Sticky clay (floral clay for holding floral foam to the sides of a container)
- Stones and marbles
- Watering cans

Instead of scattering flower vases under kitchen or bathroom sinks and in cupboards, gather them on a shelf in your decorating closet. The flower containers on the following list will cover most bouquet styles used in arranging flowers.

After you practice flower arranging *The Lazy Way* (see Chapter 14), you'll probably want to add a few more containers to this shelf. Meanwhile, these classics will fill all your basic flower-arranging needs.

QUICK ●■● PAINLESS

Carpenters have tool belts. Here's something for decorators on the move: Put the tools from your styling kit in a handy fanny pack to wear while you decorate. Miniature versions of man-size tools are all you need.

- Bud vases
- Classic glass vases
- Galvanized metal buckets and containers
- Terra cotta urns and pots
- White ironstone pitchers

Recycle attractive food containers for use as vases, and add them to your decorating closet. Wine bottles, oil and vinegar bottles, and even large-sized tin cans make wonderful and surprising vases for lazy style flower arranging.

BEAUTIFUL COLORS

A decorating closet is the perfect place to store your color box, style files, and reference books. You could also include current catalogs and magazines that inspire you.

Nearby, on the paint-supply shelf, tuck in a paint can or two of interior colors. One container could hold the basic woodwork trim color for your house. Keeping it close at hand for repairs will help you avoid wasting the time it takes to rummage through paint supplies in the garage or basement. For close-at-hand paint touch-ups, keep small amounts of your home's interior colors in glass screw-top jars.

HOUSE JEWELRY

Get back to easy. You may have forgotten that the quickest way to add mood and sparkle to a room is to light a candle. Another way is to flick the switch on a low-wattage light. To make sure you're ready to put shimmer

IF YOU'RE SO
INCLINED

Check garden stores for crocks and pots you'll find handy for flower arranging. Avoid containers with holes in the bottom for use as vases.

in a room at a moment's notice, keep these decorating gems on hand.

Candles

When you gather a supply of candles, use this classic rule of thumb when choosing colors: Choose white or a soft cream color. White candles work for every occasion, whereas colored candles are useful only for special color themes or special occasions. Use color if you like, but choose white if you want to keep things simple:

- Birthday candles
- Church and synagogue candles
- Citronella candles
- Floating candles
- Pillars
- Tea lights
- Tapers
- Votive candles

Once you've pulled together your candle supply, you'll want to collect holders and all the extras needed for lighting candles. Your candle-holder collection may be as vast as your vase collection. The best part? They're all in one place, saving you extra steps every time you throw a party or light a special moment:

- Candle pots
- Candle sticks
- Candle snuffer
- Light bulbs of various watts and sizes

QUICK ☯ PAINLESS

Add outdoor lanterns or oil lamps to your candle and holder collection. They'll be ready to go when outdoor retreats come up.

- Long-nosed lighter
- Miniature Christmas tree lights
- Votive holders

After you read "Candle Power" (Chapter 15), you'll have a dozen more ideas for items to put in your decorating closet.

Miscellaneous Supplies

Stashing these disparate items in one place isn't possible, but most of them will fit together agreeably in a cleaning carry-all, a plastic container with a handle. Lay curtain rods on a shelf and keep paper-lace doilies flattened between two pieces of cardboard:

- Cheesecloth
- Extra tension rods in a couple of sizes (18"–28", 28"–48")
- Glass cleaner
- Glue stick
- Nail-hole filler pencil
- Paper lace doilies in several sizes (coaster, plate, and platter)
- Paper towels
- Spot lifter
- Spray fabric protector
- Tack cloth
- Tung oil
- Wall-covering seam repair adhesive
- Wood finish stain marker

YOU'LL THANK YOURSELF LATER

Save time and buy yourself decorating toys while you shop for everyday supplies. Put a candle in your grocery cart, and get new color chips at the home center and a green plant at the discount store.

MUSIC TO DECORATE BY

Nothing soothes the decorating soul like great tunes. I picked a few ideas off the rack, but you'll be sure to create your own collection:

- *True Colors*, Phil Collins
- *Paint the Sky with Stars*, Enya
- *Blue*, Simply Red
- *Indigo*, Jim Donovan
- *The Agony and the Ecstasy*, Jerry Goldsmith and the Royal Scottish National Orchestra
- *Really Blue*, Tom Principato
- *No Blue Thing*, Ray Lynch
- *Dangerous Beauty*, George Fenton
- *Sapphire Dreams*, Mars Lasar

Turn on a set of decorating sounds while you read the next chapter on shortcuts.

Reward yourself with a play day after upgrading your decorating closet. Send everyone away and get out your favorite decorating files. Play a disc or tape. Sing and dance while you rearrange your decorating toys. Putter. Talk to yourself. Tell yourself how beautiful your decorating is going to be.

The Lazy Way

Getting Time on Your Side

	The Old Way	The Lazy Way
Finding tools	10–15 minutes	2 minutes
Choosing a paint color	The time it takes to get everyone's opinion	Intuitive moments by yourself
Touching up a wall	30 minutes	10 minutes
Arranging flowers	1 hour	5–15 minutes
Repairing a loose wall covering	A trip to the store	A step up the kitchen stool
Protecting a new piece of upholstery from stains	A trip to the store	A trip to the decorating closet

Chapter four

A Calendar of Decorating Tips

No matter how busy you are, don't skip this chapter. Here's why: Even if this is the only chapter you read, you'll have enough decorating ideas for an entire year. If you do nothing beyond what you find here, your results will testify to the world that you've aced Decorating 101 and can even teach everyone a thing or two.

Arranged by seasons—spring, summer, fall, and winter— these decorating short takes turn tedious everyday tasks you already do into decorating opportunities. No decorating plans, no overviews, just some off-the-cuff lazy stuff that puts fun into your ordinary days.

Also included are ideas for turning seasonal excursions into decorating expeditions. At the same time you enjoy the sights, your decorating eye will spot the makings of a beautiful tabletop or mantel. You'll want to bring ideas and pleasing objects home and extend the memory of your rich experience.

SPRING FEVER

What's this? A feeling of light headedness? A sudden impulse to create beauty and order? A crazy urge to clean?

You must be sick. Here in your down-comforted bed, now soaked in sun, you're sweating it out. The covers feel heavy and downright down, and you feverishly toss them off. Through the window, you notice how the dormant winter season has left its inevitable trail of grime and dirt. You suddenly sense a burning desire to clear away the rubbish and lighten up everything around you.

It's madness, sheer madness, but a good kind of madness. When this illness hits, my advice is this: Go with the flow, but do it *The Lazy Way*. It's the easiest decorating ride you'll ever get.

While You Clear the Decks

Throw open the windows, breathe in the air, and stretch your decorating muscles. The exercise will do you good.

■ Be a Tom Sawyer and whitewash unmatched furniture pieces. You know the story: Get the kids to help you do it. Spread newspapers over an outside work surface and coat extraneous chairs and tables with white spray paint. White-painted furniture looks clean and fresh and fits in anywhere. Another advantage is that when dissimilar pieces of furniture share a common color, they can sit together comfortably in the same room.

■ When you pick up Chinese takeout, ask for an extra quart container. Also, purchase a few fresh flowers.

After your first whirlwind clean-up, treat yourself to a variety of sprouting spring bulbs, such as daffodils, crocuses, and narcissus. Put them in appealing ceramic planters and baskets all around your home, and enjoy watching them bloom while you zoom.

The Lazy Way

At home, set the table and arrange the flowers in the extra quart container that you've partially filled with water. Voilà—a centerpiece. Ring the dinner bell and pass the Chinese, please.

- Empty and recycle. Take everything out of closets and make two stacks: The stuff you want to keep and the stuff you haven't used in a year. Wash and re-hang the clothes you'll keep. Sell or give away the rest, and take pleasure in the room-to-grow spaces you've created.

- Forget marking your garage sale stuff in advance. It takes too much time and customers always want to bargain anyway. When they ask you the price of an item, just ask them what they're willing to pay. If you like the price, agree to the deal.

- If selling your old stuff seems like too much work, give it away. People will love you for your generosity, and it'll buy you more time for things you really want to do.

- Unmake the beds for summer sleeping. Remove heavy winter comforters or blankets and flannel sheets, and replace them with a fitted cotton sheet and a lightweight summer duvet protected by a duvet cover. (A duvet is a comforter, a popular replacement for quilts and blankets, and a duvet cover is a large envelope of fabric that slips over the duvet, as a pillowcase slips over a pillow.) Cover the mattress with the fitted cotton sheet, slip the duvet inside its cover, and lay it over the fitted sheet.

QUICK ■ PALNLESS

Set the timer for 20 minutes. Sort through your dishes and pull out stray cups and plates that you never use because they don't fit any more. Give them away. You'll breathe more freely.

Set a chair in the fresh outdoors air and let the sun beam down on your head. Love *The Lazy Way*?

Although the duvet cover protects the duvet, it also serves as the top sheet, eliminating the need for one more layer. Such an arrangement keeps bed-making super simple for summer. To make the bed, just fluff the covered duvet over the bottom sheet.

While you're clearing the decks, your mind will empty itself a little, too. Celebrate the season by promising yourself you'll let go of some of the busy-busy stuff that keeps you from the really important things.

Add Magic to Mealtimes

When you go grocery shopping, treat yourself to a decorating item that isn't on your shopping list. Here are easy-to-assemble ideas to cook up while you're in the process of preparing meals.

- Select a small flat of bedding plants, such as white cascading petunias, from a springtime supermarket garden display. Without removing them from their plastic containers, fit them into a large flat-bottomed bowl or white soup tureen. Put the bowl on the dinner table as a centerpiece for a day or two. Then, plant the flowers outdoors.

- Make a "grass plot."

    1. Buy clear plastic takeout containers (from the deli counter), grass seed, and a small amount of potting soil.

    2. Fill the bottom halves of the containers with soil, plant the seed, and water gently with a spray bottle.

3. Cover the containers with their lids, and set them in a sunny location to germinate.

4. When the grass reaches a good display height, cut away the plastic lids, and arrange the "grass plots" in a line down the center of your table. If you like, place decorative items in the grass. Golf tees come to mind. If the grass grows in a few days, clip it with scissors. It'll be the easiest grass-cutting job you ever had.

Make a habit of casing the grocery store for containers you can use as flower vases, paper dinnerware that makes a pretty party happen, or food you can assemble into a delectable, edible centerpiece.

THOSE LAZY DAYS OF SUMMER

You lie back on the grass and watch the puffy white clouds roll by. At night, you stare at the stars. Perhaps you can take a break and check out the decorating scene in your living or family room.

While You Kick Back on the Sofa

Consider rearranging the room—okay, maybe not now, but sometime in the future.

▪ In the heat of the summer months, turn your back—and your sofa—on the indoors. Arrange the seating with a view to the windows and the out-of-doors. Find places where you can lean large framed mirrors to reflect window light into the room. It brings the great outdoors inside.

IF YOU'RE SO
INCLINED

Loosen your decorating look by leaning a print or a painting against the wall, rather than hanging it. The casual touch is part of the charm of lazy ease.

- Strip down for summer. Change the heavy plush or pile rugs in your rooms to sisal for a cooler look and feel. You can also let your floors go barefoot, leaving them without rugs.

- Simplify the view. Remove the distractions of too many colorful paintings or pictures on the walls, and replace them with mirrors to reflect light and views of the out-of-doors.

Kicking back on the sofa sounds lazy, but sometimes, it's just plain necessary while you plan your next decorating move. I do my best thinking in a prone position. In that relaxed state, visualization takes place, and once I can picture what I'm going to do, getting up and doing it is a piece of cake.

While You Put the Shrimp on the Bar-B

Add a decorative item to the menu while you turn the meat on the grill. Here are a couple ideas you can assemble with one hand tied behind your back (or tied to the grill).

- Create a tabletop centerpiece on the picnic table with galvanized yard and garden containers, such as watering cans, French flowerpots, and farm buckets. Put a green plant in one of the containers for a focal point in the arrangement. Let rain collect in the other containers, and use it to water the green plant on dry days.

QUICK ◉ PAINLESS

For the greatest impact, when you arrange your green plants, mass them together rather than scatter them across the floor.

- Hang lanterns on a summer balcony or deck or in the trees near a hammock. They can be as simple as a string of electrical lights with decorative covers or containers that are powered by candles.

- Pretend it's Christmas in July. Hang hundreds of miniature Christmas tree lights in trees for night-time midsummer magic.

- Bring home a potted flowering tree to spruce up the patio or balcony.

AUTUMN DAZE

The leaves are falling. You can hear them whispering in the autumn wind, changing colors and directions, growing down instead of up. You drive down the road at the peak of the season to catch their final beauty on the wing.

While You Wander the Country Roads

When the first leaves of autumn scatter in the urgent wind, celebrate the passing season by preparing for the next. Capture fleeting moments with a gathering of burnished reds and oranges.

- Stop at a farm stand to pick up extra pumpkins or squash, and turn them into flower vases or serving dishes. When you get them home, cut away their tops, carve out the seeds and loose pulp, and take them to the table full of flowers or mashed potatoes.

Hang out on the balcony every starry summer night that you can. Take a decorating break. All you need to make the occasion special are a couple candles, a little music, and a friend or two.

The Lazy Way

- For pumpkin place cards at your Thanksgiving table, follow these steps:

  1. Gather fall leaves and miniature pumpkins.

  2. Loop a ribbon around each pumpkin stem, insert the leaf stems inside the loop, and tighten the ribbon.

  3. Tie the ribbon in a bow, and slide the paper-punched corner of a place card onto the ribbon, tucking it up under the bow.

  4. Place the pumpkin place card to the left of the water glasses at your table.

- Another mini idea: Pumpkin lights. Carve round holes in the tops of miniature pumpkins that are wide enough to hold votive candles or tea lights.

While you're taking that stroll around the park in the fall, remember to look down. Pick up the most beautiful dry leaf specimens you can find (I'm particularly fond of huge sycamore leaves) and take them home to dry out a little more. Stack them loosely, and slip them inside a brown paper bag. They can add a decorative touch to almost anything, and they make great ornaments for a Christmas tree.

While You Haunt the Flea Markets

Autumn is a great time to wander around outdoor flea markets. Arrive early to scan the entire market for an overview. Make notes of the spots where you encountered objects that jumped up to say, "Take me home!"

IF YOU'RE SO INCLINED

Gather dried leaves and slip them under the glass of a vanity or dining-room table.

- Choose one special object rather than a host of little things. One unusually shaped bowl elevated on a stand at home will be more dramatic and interesting than a number of small pieces.

- When you're considering choices, look for a piece to add to a collection you already have, rather than the hodge-podge of things you probably don't know what to do with.

- If you're starting a collection, buy pretty and practical. Dinnerware is a good choice because it's completely functional. Mass your finds for display in a cupboard rather than scattering them around the house. Bring them to the table for special occasions.

Page through magazines for ideas on how people display their dinnerware collections. You might find a fresh way you can display your flea market finds on the wall, in a cupboard, on a ledge, or as a tabletop centerpiece.

LONG, LEISURELY WINTER NIGHTS

Short, sunny days and long, cold nights leave more hours in the day for close encounters with home entertainment of the redecorating kind.

Get That Fireplace Feeling

Whether you have a fireplace or not, these tips will give you that close-to-the fire feeling.

No fireplace? The good news is that you can fake it. It's a lot easier than creating and keeping up a real

YOU'LL THANK YOURSELF LATER

Limit your dinnerware collection to a color scheme you can live with, such as red and cream ware, blue and white china, or white and gold porcelain.

working fireplace. To create the look of a real fireplace, follow these steps:

1. Purchase a fireplace surround from a salvage yard and move it into your house.

2. Fill the firebox opening of the fireplace with a large mirror to reflect the room and whatever you place on the floor in front of the mirror.

3. To create the look of fire in the firebox, lay a string of miniature Christmas tree lights in a loose arrangement on the floor and plug it in. The mirror will reflect twice the light.

For fireside dining or an evening of cards, pull a round patio table out of storage and place it in front of the fireplace. Cover it with a cloth to hide its patio appearance, and pull up small dining or folding chairs for your guests.

Take advantage of the mood and furniture arrangement you've created. Wrap up in a luxury throw, read a good book, and enjoy your feeling of accomplishment.

While You Decorate for the Holidays

The mere fact that guests are coming can add a lot of stress to your life. Relax. These ideas will spur you on to refurbish those unkempt corners and add charm to your home.

▧ Assemble a guest room:

1. Clear out an extra room, packing its contents into storage boxes that will slide under the bed.

Arrange chairs in a circular grouping around the fire and bring out luxurious throws of dark velvets and touch-me fabrics. Relax in the fire's warm glow with your favorite drink, and admire the work you did.

The Lazy Way

2. Angle the bed to avoid a boxy feel in the room and place a hamper at the end of it for extra blankets.

3. Put together a bedside stand with a small table, a lamp, flowers, and a basket of luxury items for the bath.

◾ Create a dazzling side-table centerpiece.

1. Spray a large grapevine wreath white.

2. When it's dry, lay it on the table and twine two white strings of miniature Christmas tree lights around it.

3. Place a large white porcelain wash bowl in the center of the wreath and trail the rest of the light string into it.

4. Fill the bowl with large glass ornament balls for a dazzling bowl of light.

◾ For extra dining surfaces, place small round decorator tables in front of a sofa.

◾ If you have a four-season porch, dress your garden furniture in dining finery, covering tables with pretty cloths and slipping fabric and swags over the backs of chairs.

Treat yourself to down time before everyone arrives or after everyone leaves. That might mean a long soak in the tub behind closed doors. If you're not the bathtub type, schedule a body massage, or a nap in front of the TV.

IF YOU'RE SO
INCLINED

For instant luxury in your guest room, dress the bed in two bed skirts, one slightly longer than the other.

Is It Over?

Not until the fat lady sings, and I don't see her anywhere; do you? Life goes on. After the holidays, you find yourself in the cooler, deeper months of the year, wishing for the warmer ones to return. To brighten the dark post-holiday months, use candles and low-lamp lights to set a warm, intimate mood in the house. Add some warm decorative touches for Valentine's Day, and consider Groundhog Day an advance celebration of the coming spring. Before long, you'll notice crocuses and daffodils popping up in the grocery store. Take some home for your dinner table.

Getting Time on Your Side

	The Old Way	The Lazy Way
Creating a guest room	1 week	1 day
Making your bed	5 minutes	1 minute
Finding extra storage space	No time	Anytime
Finding hammock time	Rarely	Often
Creating a pretty dinner table	1 hour	10 minutes
Cleaning out the fireplace	(Censored)	Never

Easy Ways Out of Decorating Messes

Football and redecorating are about the same when it comes to getting the results you want and cleaning up without knocking yourself out. Redecorating is like a game that's planned and visualized in your mind long before it takes place. The first rule: The best offense is a good defense. The second? Four yards and a cloud of dust. (That's football talk for achieving the goal a little at a time.)

Stick to the clean-up plan, hitting debris head on and clearing it away as you go. If you let the mess get out of hand, you'll feel like a loser knee-deep in torn-up turf.

Browse this chapter for tips that will keep you ahead of the clean-up game. I've organized my best *Lazy Ways* into several types of projects that might interest you: Easy painting, wall papering with borders, simple woodworking, furniture and fabric upkeep, *Lazy Way* flower arranging, and burning candles that might leave messes.

First up to bat? The painting game.

Use latex paint and buy no-splatter paint rollers for painting walls. They'll save you clean-up time like no other materials and tools available. Use a quality cutting-in brush that won't scatter brush hairs in your paint or on the wall.

PAINT SPLATTERS BE GONE

Imagine the worst mess and prepare for it. If you do, it probably won't happen and you can walk away from the scene feeling like a pro.

Here's how to get around the bases with the least amount of resistance:

▪ Avoid oil-based paints: Whenever possible, avoid paint products that require cleaning up with mineral spirits. It's a messy ordeal you can leave to painters who love sticky paints and the results they can achieve with them. Select water-based paints that clean up easily with water.

▪ Use easy-clean foam brushes: For small paint touch-ups, substitute easy-to-clean foam brushes and paint pads for bristle paintbrushes that take longer to wash up. Just run water through them, give them a quick squeeze, and set them up to dry. Just throw them away if they're beyond saving. They didn't cost that much in the first place.

▪ Easy paint protection: Use non-splatter wall-painting tools so you don't need to cover your floors and furniture with cumbersome drop cloths or yards of plastic sheeting. Just flatten a corrugated cardboard box and slide it along the floor in front of the wall section you're painting.

▪ Spray paint outside: Work outdoors to spray paint furniture or small accessories. A week later, the grass will have grown, and you can mow away the signs of paint.

- Bristle-brush clean-up: Clean your brush in warm water and swirl it against a bar of oil soap until the bristles are sudsy right up to the heel. Rinse and flex the bristles under water until the water runs clear. Give the bristles a squeeze with your hand.

- Be orderly: Hang your paintbrushes and rollers on nails or hooks after you've finished a project and cleaned them.

Store your paint supplies in their designated places so you'll be sure to find them quickly the next time you need them. If you can manage a smooth game of paint clean-up, you can manage anything. Now for the easy stuff.

PASTE PATROL

When you've committed yourself to a little wallpaper hanging, you've also committed yourself to an easy clean-up process. By nature, hanging a wall-covering border is a clean operation. Water is part of the process anyway, and everything about it wants to be neat and tidy. It's just a matter of not getting caught with a few sticky pieces of paper hanging about in the wrong places.

Here's how to keep your paper-hanging process in perfect order so that your clean-up is over within two or three minutes of finishing the project:

- Choose washable wall-covering borders for easy cleaning.

- When hanging a wall-covering border, prepare it on a washable work surface. A kitchen counter is a

A COMPLETE WASTE OF TIME

The 3 Worst Things to Do When Cleaning Up Paint:

1. Put your brush in a tin can of water.

2. Leave your paintbrush lying open to the air while you take a break.

3. Let the paintbrush dry and cake up with paint.

good candidate because it's washable and near the sink.

- Clean as you go, keeping a small bucket of warm rinse water handy. Use it to rinse out the cloth you use to smooth the wall-covering border and wipe away the excess paste.

- Throw away paper scraps as you cut them so they don't pile up or get stuck to other surfaces. Collect them in a paper bag or plastic-lined wastebasket you keep close by.

- Clean your scissors when your project is finished.

- Store your wall-covering tools in the predetermined spot in your decorating closet, ready for use the next time you get a paper-hanging whim.

Although wall-covering messes are naturally washed up as you go, doing a project that involves wood often leaves a trail of dust. Sometimes, you need to keep power tools in line.

SCORE ONE FOR SAFETY

Of all the redecorating projects, the ones involving wood tools need the most organization and orderly steps. Keeping your work surfaces neat will keep you from tangling with electrical cords and dangerous cutting blades.

These suggestions might be more than you need for simple *Lazy Way* wood drilling and refinishing projects, but it doesn't hurt to have a few extra precautions and tips under your redecorating belt:

QUICK ☜☞ *PAINLESS*

Buy a package of *cloth* diapers for cleaning up decorating messes. Keep them in your decorating closet so they don't get confused with regular household cleaning equipment.

- Choose a rough work surface: For projects that require cutting, sanding, and drilling wood, choose a work surface that can take a beating. Locate it in a place where it will create the least amount of dust in the house, especially near electronic equipment.

- Bust the dust: Handy vacuums are perfect for cleaning sawdust and wood debris. A portable battery-powered hand vacuum will take care of most decorating messes in the house. If you get into big woodworking projects, a shop vacuum is the right clean-up tool.

- Sweep up: Pull small messes into piles at regular intervals to avoid tracking sawdust through the house. Do a thorough cleanup when the project is finished so an old mess doesn't add to your next one.

- Prevent dust damage: Spread a plastic drop cloth over sensitive or hard-to-clean items to save hours of clean-up and costly repairs.

If woodworking and furniture have any clean-up problems in common, it's dust—natural, blowing-in-the-wind dust or dust created by power machines. Here's what to do about the stuff that comes blowing in through the cracks and vents in your house and raises havoc with your wood-surfaced furnishings.

POLISH AND SHINE

You probably hire someone to do your floor and furniture refinishing, but the upkeep of your wood paneling,

YOU'LL THANK YOURSELF LATER

Cover electronic equipment when a dusty decorative project, such as getting your floors professionally refinished, is being done at your house. You don't need the added expense, not to mention the inconvenience, of cleaning up after an electronic tragedy.

Buy yourself a handy lit-
tle cordless, hand-held
vacuum cleaner that you
recharge on a wall-hung
storage rack. It's worth
its weight in gold for
quick dusting and small
jobs.

cabinetry, and floors, as well as your upholstered furniture, is something that only you will guard.

Despite the list of clean-up tips and cautions that follows, my best advice is this: Moderation in all things.
Don't overdo your cleaning (love that *Lazy Way*!), or
you'll ruin your house and everything in it. My friend
Karla, the queen of clean, will testify to that piece of wisdom. Shortly after she became a new bride, she moved
into her first home and began keeping house with a
vengeance. (She always does everything with passion.)

She made a career of keeping up her house: Monday
was baking, cooking, and cleaning-the-kitchen day;
Tuesday was for vacuuming the whole house and dusting
every surface in it. Wednesday was reserved for laundry
and re-doing all the beds, guests or not. On Thursdays,
she scrubbed and waxed vinyl and stone floors, even the
front stone walk outside the door. On Fridays, she
shopped for the week's groceries and re-organized every
food storage unit in the house. She'd call me on the
phone and tell me about every accomplishment as if she
were getting her master's degree in home-keeping.

A year later, she called me in tears. She'd worn the
finish off all her carpets, abused her stone floors with
super cleaning agents, washed her curtains, drapes, and
bedding to within shreds of their serviceable lives, and
was now giving me advice: Don't clean too much. It's a
bad thing.

Her point was well taken (not that I had any trouble
accepting it). I pass these easy-does-it tips on to you:

- Easy dust it: Take it easy when you dust your furniture. Don't overload wood surfaces with sticky, dulling dust repellants that build up. A soft towel and damp cloth is a natural, non-abrasive way to clean.

- Clean gently: Oil soap is a gentle cleaner that doesn't leave dulling residue and is kind to wood and hands. Use it on wood floors, paneling, cabinetry, painted wood, tables, chairs, and bookcases. It's also wonderful for non-wood surfaces, such as no-wax floors, ceramic tile, painted surfaces, leather, vinyl, and even stained laundry.

- Go non-abrasive: Vacuum and mop wood floors with mild non-abrasive cleaners. Never use hot water or pour it directly onto the floor. Install felt pads under the feet of furniture to prevent them from scratching your floors.

Apply the moderation rule to these rules for caring for the fabrics in your house.

HOLDING THE FABRIC LINE

Remember the phrase, "Whoever dies with the most fabric wins?" You won't be a winner if you don't care for your favorite tablecloths, runners, and napkins after you've used them. Here's how to keep them ready to go at a moment's notice:

- Keep them in perfect or near-perfect condition. After they've had a workout, remove stains and wash or dry-clean them and return them to the drawers and shelves you've reserved for them.

QUICK ⬛ *PAINLESS*

Follow the golden cleaning rule: Clean only as much as you would like to be cleaned yourself. Too much cleaning abuses and scrapes away good surfaces.

- Store everyday fabrics in dry, dark closets and drawers to avoid mildew stains and bleaching sunlight.

- Wrap heirloom fabrics in acid-free tissue, not plastic. Fabrics need to breathe air to keep their fibers from weakening and breaking down.

- Buy upholstered furniture with stain-resistant finishes. Or apply your own fabric protector by following the instructions on the fabric protector container.

- Blot spills as soon as possible after they occur. Home remedies for removing stains on fabric are effective to varying degrees, but none will get out every stain. Dab stain removers on the edges of the stain and work toward the center, and then blot with a clean cloth.

- Have professional cleaners remove stains you can't.

When it comes to keeping up fabrics—especially the casual, natural canvas so typical of *Lazy Way* decorating—I'm particularly fond of spraying fabric protector on new and newly cleaned fabrics. There's nothing more gratifying than to watch a nasty spill bead up on the surface of a fabric and wait to be carried away on a paper towel. That's lazy style at its best.

FLOWER POWER

Ahhh…flowers. Supple, easy, and lightweight—and wet. If you don't plan for flower-arranging clean-up, extra leaves and trimmings will mound up in a hurry, clogging your sink and spilling damp messes onto surfaces where you don't want them.

Once every summer, bring your white linens out for a day. After you wash them, treat them (and yourself) to a sun bath on the grass or outdoor deck. The sun will lighten and brighten your whitening efforts while you lie around. Imagine what the neighbors will say!

The Lazy Way

Actually, there's nothing to it. Just keep these suggestions in mind when you do your flower arranging:

- Keep a tall, plastic florist bucket to hold flowers when you bring them in from the garden or home from the store. Remove the florist's paper coverings from your flowers, snip off the ends of their stems, and stand them in the water-filled bucket until you're ready to arrange them.

- To keep water spills at a minimum, work at the kitchen sink (put in the drainage stopper to keep small cuttings from clogging the drain) to arrange your flowers. Pull excess leaves off stems, letting them and your stem trimmings fall into the sink. When you've finished with the flowers, gather the trimmings into a wastebasket and clear the sink of residue.

- Wash and dry your cutting shears when you're finished. Store them in the place you've given them in your decorating closet.

If you're cleaning up after arranging flowers, you're probably having a party and lighting candles to make sure the occasion feels like one. Candles are fabulous, but....

Have you ever watched the candles at a party burn down? At some point, you get alarmed enough to point out to the hostess that her darling tree-shaped candles are spilling over the edges of their tiny tree-trunk containers and getting dark green wax all over her best linen tablecloth.

QUICK ⬛ PAINLESS

Keep the water in your flower vase fresh so that mineral deposits don't build up inside the vase. Rinse it after use and store.

How about the time your own candles toppled over in the chandelier above the dining room table? That's when you added a little caution to your candle-lighting customs.

WHEN THE PARTY'S OVER

Cleaning up dripped or spilled candle wax is a downer after the candles have set the mood for a really good time. It's like the morning after. These pain relievers will help.

Hot Tonics for Spilled Wax

Candle wax gone over the line? Push it back with these hot and cold wax clean-ups:

- To remove wax from the bottoms of metal candleholders, put them in the freezer for an hour and use a butter knife to gently scrape away the wax. You can also heat them in a warm oven and wipe away the remaining residue with a clean rag.

- To remove wax from common glass candleholders that have no metal parts, put them in the microwave for a minute or two. Then, wipe out the wax with a paper towel. To polish them, dip the candleholders in a pan of hot water and wipe away the residue with more towels.

- To remove wax from tablecloths, let the wax cool thoroughly before you peel away as much of it as possible. Then, place the drip area on a paper-towel–covered surface, cover with several more paper towels, and iron over them to remove the rest of the wax.

To remove wax from wood surfaces, gently scrape it away with a cloth-covered butter knife.

Taking preventive measures for candle burning is better than dealing with the heartbreak of spilled wax and candles dripping all over your magic kingdom. Why not do what you can to avoid having to use the clean-up tips here.

An Ounce of Wax-Ident Prevention

Here are some steps you can take to head off candle-burning problems before they happen:

- Plan ahead for dripping candles by placing them on deep coasters or plates. Buy candles in glass containers so the wax can't spill over the edges.

- Avoid buying cleverly shaped party candles that stand on tiny bases. When the candle is larger than the holder, you are looking at a candle accident waiting to happen.

- Use dripless candles in chandeliers or wall-hung candle holders.

- To keep candles from flopping over in their holders, wrap bits of tin foil around their bottoms before inserting them securely into their candlesticks or stands.

Don't let all these wax precautions keep you from lighting candles. If you don't learn anything else from this book, know this: The light of a candle will add more to your redecorating scheme than any other lazy trick in the book.

YOU'LL THANK YOURSELF LATER

Make a habit of checking the candles you're burning. If you're involved with a lot of guests, ask someone to help you watch them.

Getting Time on Your Side

	The Old Way	The Lazy Way
Paint clean-up	20 minutes	10 minutes
Wallpaper clean-up	20 minutes	5 minutes
Flower arranging clean-up	10 minutes	5 minutes
Candle clean-up	Scratch and scrape	Melt your troubles away
Garage sale clean-up	Sell it	Give it away
Fabric clean-up	Scrub-a-dub-dub	A little dab'll do ya

Decorating Lite: Fuss-Free Ways to Beautiful Rooms

Are You Too Lazy to Read "Decorating Lite: Fuss-Free Ways to Beautiful Rooms?"

1 You think a flower arrangement is a deal for regular deliveries from the florist. ☐ yes ☐ no

2 Your impulse to redecorate is strongest when you stain the rug and must move a chair to cover it. ☐ yes ☐ no

3 Your idea of stretching out your living space is moving more junk into the garage. ☐ yes ☐ no

Shortcuts to Covering Your Walls

So you think painting a wall sounds like work. You'd rather climb Mt. Everest than scale the walls of your living room with a paintbrush or a long strip of wallpaper. Covering your furniture and floors and wobbling on a shaky ladder to reach the upper corners of the room is not your idea of a good time.

I'm with you.

I love my home, and I want it to look good, but I don't want to spend all my time and energy redecorating. I've figured out how to make it easier and get it done faster. One option is to get someone else to do the basics (the drudgery parts) for me. Then, I can come along and do the lightweight, fun decorating myself.

Another way to keep decorating fun is to limit it to short projects that are an enhancement to life, not a painful drain on time. That's particularly important when it comes to decorating the larger areas of your home—such as walls. Walls are walls, straight up. They can seem like mountains to climb, but you can turn them into something fun to do. In this chapter, I show you ways to decorate your walls with small amounts of paint and wallpaper that will make covering them feel more like a walk in the park than a drawn-out marathon run.

LAZY SCHEMER

Who said the only way to paint a room or hang wall covering is to cover every wall in the place? That's the old-fashioned way. Leave it behind, and learn how to transform the look of your home in far less time. Paint just one wall (or part of a wall), or hang a snappy die-cut wallpaper border, and get superb decorating results that make it look like you did a lot of work. I'll tell you how to do it.

Buy Pre-Mixed, Pre-Cut, and Pre-Pasted

Nothing else will do. Baby yourself with the laziest materials on the shelf, and you'll cut the decorating work to shreds. Lazy-does-it means that you follow these tips:

- Use water-based latex paints that clean up with water.
- Use non-splattering paint rollers so you don't have to cover the world with drop cloths before you start painting.
- Buy pre-cut and pre-pasted wallpaper borders (not double rolls of 27-inch-wide paper), and dip them in a bucket of warm water.

Add a few handy cutting, measuring, and cleaning tools, and you're home free.

Love That Latex

Latex paints have gained popularity over solvent-based paints because they're easy to apply, less expensive, and friendly to the environment. Another benefit is that they clean up with water rather than chemical solvents and thinners. Semi-gloss (slight sheen) latex paints wear better than flat latex colors.

You can paint the accent walls and color blocks that follow with flat latex paint.

PLAN TO GO PARTIAL

The lazy plan cuts traditional painting down to the simple (and elegant) essentials. With paint and wallpaper, you can get dramatic decorating done by

- Painting an accent wall.
- Giving one wall in the room a block of glorious color.

When it comes to hanging wallpaper, go for the borders only. They're powerful enough to put style in any room if you hang them in just the right places.

When I was a set designer for a national home magazine, I had ample opportunities for lazy scheming. My job was to create interiors for readers who wanted ideas for window treatments, floor and wall decorations, furniture fix-ups, and room and accessory arranging. A photographer would photograph the sets, and the pictures became magazine pages. As I planned the sets, I specified

A COMPLETE WASTE OF TIME

The 3 Worst Things to Do with Latex Paint:

1. Brush it over dirty surfaces.

2. Buy poor-quality latex paint. The price may enchant you, but it will cost you in the long run.

3. Apply it with a natural bristle brush that will soak up water, dry out the paint, and injure the brush.

QUICK 🔘 PAINLESS

The beauty of paint is that if you don't like the results, you can always make it disappear. Just paint it out.

what colors and wallpapers should appear on the walls, and the photo studio staff assembled them for me. After the furniture movers added the furniture and walked away, I was left to "fluff" the set (make it soft and inviting) for the camera.

Okay, I admit it; I got more opportunities to decorate *The Lazy Way* than most people have in a lifetime. But look at it this way: Now I can pass along the tricks of the trade to you.

SPEED PAINTING WADE'S WAY

Here's one of my favorite studio stories. One day, a photographer and I arrived on a set that was the subject of a magazine article on focal-point walls and discovered that the accent wall prepared for it had been obliterated mistakenly by a well-meaning painter. The light was perfect, and if we were to capture the picture, we had to do it within an hour. The pressure was on to somehow make it work.

Enter Wade, the painter who'd made the error. He was upstairs in the house, overheard our discussion, and from a balcony above, said, "I'm the painter who did it. If you can get me the paint, I'll paint it right back!" We did, and he did, and here's how.

Working with easy-to-apply, quick-dry latex paint that cleans up with water, Wade *cut in* (*cutting in* is paint lingo for carefully brushing on three-inch-wide paint margins) around the edges of the wall to prepare for fast-and-easy rolling.

With his non-splatter, synthetic-sleeved roller attached to a 30-inch extension handle, Wade dipped into a bucket of paint, distributed it evenly on the roller, and covered the wall between the cut-in margins in 20 minutes flat. The only protection he used from possible paint spills was a flattened corrugated box that he slid along the base molding in front of him. He said he could be sure that the non-splatter roller would keep the paint from landing on the carpet. After that, I knew painting a wall Wade's way could be called painting a wall *The Lazy Way*.

The Accent's on Quick

Let's say you're living in a space with basic beige or white walls, and you'd like to punch up the color scheme a little or give the room a focal point. An accent wall, a single wall painted in a contrasting color, will do the job. Use the magic word, paint—the least expensive decorating material and the fastest way to create redecorating impact—and you're almost there. Check the accent wall illustration to see how it looks, and follow the instructions.

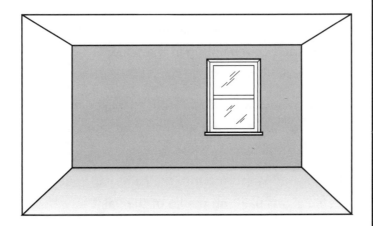

To create an accent wall, paint one wall in a color that contrasts with the other walls in the room.

Get a non-splatter roller such as the one Wade used (made by Sherwin Williams), and you'll have nothing to clean up. Spend the time you saved eating takeout and admiring your work.

Here's what you need to paint an accent wall:

- Plastic drop cloth
- One gallon of custom-mixed latex paint of your choice
- Paint stir-stick
- Two-inch-wide, angled, synthetic-bristle paintbrush
- Kitchen step ladder
- Paint tray
- Non-splatter, synthetic-sleeved roller with a handle that will accept an extension handle
- A 30-inch extension handle for the paint roller

Put on some decorating music before you take these steps to cover a wall.

1. Push your furniture back from the wall you intend to paint.

2. Cover the floor in front of the wall with a plastic drop cloth.

3. Place the kitchen stool in front of the wall where you can begin painting at the upper-left corner of the wall.

4. Open the paint can and stir it to make sure it's evenly mixed. Pour a small amount into the paint tray so you can carry it with you.

5. Dip your paintbrush into the paint and wipe off the excess paint on the lip of the paint tray. Use this stroke every time you replenish the brush.

YOU'LL THANK YOURSELF LATER

When you choose a color from the paint-chip rack at the paint store, go one or two steps lighter than the first color you choose. Paint gets a lot more intense on the wall than it appears on the paint chip.

6. Apply the paint to the uppermost corner of the wall and carefully work the ends of the brush along the edge of the wall where it meets the ceiling. Paint down about three inches. This is called cutting in.

7. Cut in three-inch margins around the top, sides, and bottom of the wall. Then, retire your paintbrush. The hard part is over.

8. Set your paint tray on the drop cloth in front of the wall. Pour a cup or two of paint into your paint tray. See that ribbed bottom in the tray? That's for distributing the paint evenly on your paint roller.

9. Add the extension handle to the handle on your paint roller.

10. Press the paint roller into the paint, and roll it back and forth on the ribbed surface of the paint tray until the paint is evenly distributed.

11. Use long, up-and-down roller strokes that overlap each other. (Overlapping strokes clear away paint trails your roller might leave.) Roll paint across the wall, replenishing the roller and paint tray as it's needed.

12. Wash up with water when you're finished.

A COMPLETE WASTE OF TIME

The 3 Worst Things to Do When Buying a Paint Roller:

1. Buy one with a cardboard core that absorbs moisture and crumbles with washing.

2. Pick one with a handle that has to be screwed off for sleeve replacement.

3. Choose one with grips without threads for attaching an extension handle.

Child's Play: Give Your Room a Color Block

You can put a lot of style on your walls by painting a single band or block of color on a pale or neutral wall to create a stunning focal point. If you can paint an accent wall, you can paint a block of color on a wall instead of painting the whole thing. The only difference is that the edges of a color block are marked off with painter's tape, the low-tack masking tape manufactured especially for wall painting. It makes quick work of cutting in around the edges of the color block.

Here are four ways to color-block a wall:

- Partial accent wall: A partial accent wall on one side or end of the room can be painted in a fairly strong color. Buy only a quart or two because you'll use only a small amount. Check the photograph section in this book to see this partial accent wall.

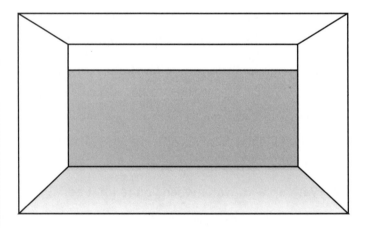

For a partial accent wall, paint a contrasting color on the wall from the floor up to a line that falls 24 inches below the ceiling.

- One-color accent band: Use a single color to make a vertical accent band on a windowless wall.

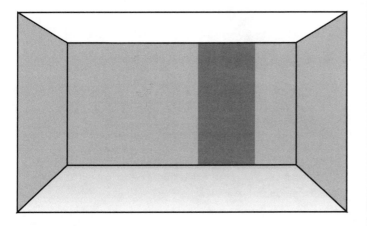

On a windowless wall, paint a one-color accent band from floor to ceiling.

- Two-color accent band: For a two-color accent band on light-colored walls, paint the lighter accent color over the entire accent band section. After the light color dries for two days, paint the darker band over the center of it.

- Two-color banded wall: Using the proportions of the diagram, paint the darker-toned sections on a lighter-colored wall of the same hue.

You can add a beautiful block of color to a room in less time than it takes to paint an entire wall. Visualize it first. (That means sitting around and thinking about it for a long time before actually getting up and doing something about it.) You'll be surprised at how rapidly you complete the project when you take the time to

Add to your painting pleasure by playing Enya's *Paint the Sky With Stars* CD. Paint to the rhythm. It's almost like dancing.

The Lazy Way

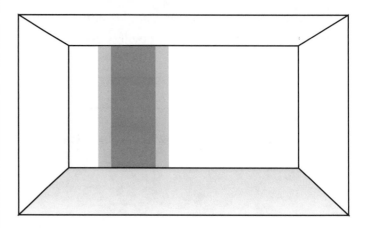

Paint a two-color accent band from floor to ceiling to create a stunning focal-point wall.

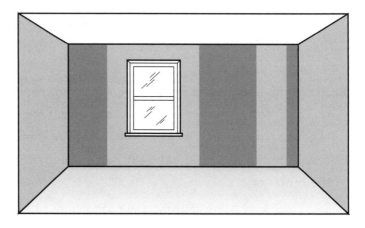

Repeat a color band in different widths on a plain-colored wall.

visualize. It's like planning a football play before you go out on the field.

To paint a color-blocked wall, you'll need

- Long straight-edged level you've borrowed from a woodworking friend (or lengthen a small level by putting a yardstick on top of it to extend the line)

- Yardstick
- Pencil
- Painter's tape
- A quart or two of latex paint
- Two-inch-wide synthetic-bristle paintbrush
- Paint tray
- Six-inch-wide paint roller

Now, play that field of color.

1. Mark the width and height of the blocks or bands on the wall with a pencil. Then, using the straight edge of the level, extend the marks from side to side or from ceiling to floor to create perimeter lines. Watch the bubble in the level to create perfectly plumb lines. These lines mark the edges of the color block and the place where you will lay the edge of the painter's tape.

2. Lay painter's tape along the pencil lines around the color block. Smooth the edges of the tape with your finger to be sure it's well adhered to the wall so paint won't ooze under the edges of the tape and ruin your perfect edge.

3. Open your paint can and stir with a stir-stick to make sure it's well mixed.

4. Dip your paintbrush into the can, and smooth away the excess on one side by brushing it against the lip of the can. Use this stroke every time you take paint from the can.

YOU'LL THANK YOURSELF LATER

Wear disposable plastic gloves while painting to save wear and tear on your hands or manicure.

5. Beginning at the inside edge of the tape (it's okay to get paint on it), use brush strokes that move away from the tape, not toward it. (This will keep paint from going under the tape.) Brush three-inch margins of paint around the edges of the color block. Retire your paintbrush.

6. Pour a cup or two of paint in your paint tray and distribute it evenly on the roller by rolling it against the ribbed surface in the bottom of the tray.

7. Apply the paint between the brushed-on margins by rolling it on in overlapping strokes.

8. Carefully remove the painter's tape while the paint is still wet.

9. Clean up with soap and water.

HEAD FOR THE BORDER

Spare yourself the agony of papering whole walls. You can hang wallpaper border and still get a wall-covering look you love. Apprehensive? It's really a matter of handling the product and feeling its weightlessness. The next time you're in a home center or paint store that carries wall covering, compare a roll of regular wall covering to a roll of border. That'll give you a picture of how easy and stress-free decorating a wall can be.

Take home a roll of wallpaper border just to get comfortable with it. It'll cost you between $5 and $10 to unroll a strip at home and tape it up tentatively. Then you'll know whether you want to commit to pasting it up permanently.

When you browse through wall-covering books, you'll be struck by the variety of borders available. The most notable borders are the new ones with a die-cut edge on one side. This shapely cut edge follows the printed design of the border and gives you a new decorating opportunity without any additional work.

You can buy two types of borders:

- Directional: When you look at the designs, note how some of them have a definite "this way up" look. These are directional borders and must be hung in only one direction, the right one.

- Non-directional: Of the two border types, non-directional borders are more flexible and easier to use because you can hang them right side up, upside down, or sideways, and they'll never look wrong.

You can use wallpaper borders as a

- Frieze (a decorative band) at the top of a room
- Wainscot, a dado, or lower portion of a wall
- Floor molding
- Window frame

Directional borders are good for treatments that wrap around a room on the same level, whereas non-directional borders work well around window frames.

At the end of this chapter, you'll find a set of step-by-step instructions for hanging wallpaper borders that you

A COMPLETE WASTE OF TIME

The 3 Worst Surfaces on Which to Apply Wall Covering:

1. Smooth, shiny surfaces you haven't sanded

2. Dirty, greasy walls

3. Unprimed walls

QUICK ◼ PAINLESS

To calculate the amount of border paper you'll need, simply measure the distance you plan to cover and add two extra yards. Then, check the wallpaper book for the length of each roll, and do the painless math.

can use for any or all of the four wall treatment ideas that follow.

Frieze It

Get with the Greeks—those guys who had time to carve and paint great decorative borders around the tops of their rooms at the Parthenon. There's just one big difference: You can do yours without all the sweat and strain, thanks to the beautiful architectural and floral borders printed by manufacturers of wallpaper.

For a frieze, you can use either a directional or non-directional border because you're going to hang it only around the top of your room. Just be sure you pick one that will look right hanging downward. Position it directly under the ceiling molding (if you have one) or tuck it right up at the top of the wall where it meets the ceiling.

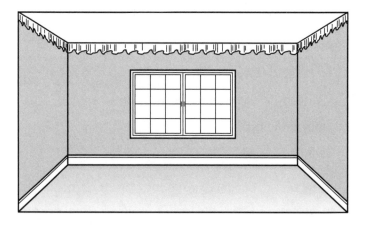

Hang a wallpaper border at the top of a room to create a decorative frieze.

Wow! It's a Wainscot Record

In a quarter of the time it takes to hang a wood-paneled or wallpaper wainscot, you can have the look of a wainscot with a six- to nine-inch-wide border.

A wainscot is a *dado* (the lower portion of an interior wall) that's finished in either wallpaper, fabric, paint, or wood. After the material has been attached to the wall, it's usually topped off with a trim of wood molding called a *chair rail.*

The average height for a wainscot is 30 to 33 inches, including the trim. If you hang a wallpaper border with its top edge at a 33-inch height in a room with painted walls, you'll have the look of a wainscot.

To prepare for hanging the border, you'll need to measure and mark off the line that will guide you.

You'll need

■ Tape measure

■ Pencil

■ Carpenter's level with straight edge

You'll need your tape measure first.

1. Measure 33 inches up the wall from the floor with your tape measure.

2. Mark the height with your pencil.

3. Place the carpenter's level at the mark, check that the bubble is level, and extend the mark with your pencil using the straight edge of the level as a guide.

IF YOU'RE SO
INCLINED

Double the border and double the fun. Sometimes, two borders hung together are better than one.

4. Move the level along the wall (watch the bubble) and extend the line around the room.

5. Place the top edge of the border along your pencil line.

Swing Low, Sweet Border

I never considered hanging a wallpaper border at the *bottom* of a wall until I saw someone else do it. It's stunning in a hallway that leads into the next room.

You can hang a border at the bottom of the room by reversing the process for a wainscot and pasting it above the top edge of the base molding. You'll need a non-directional border or a directional border that looks good going upward.

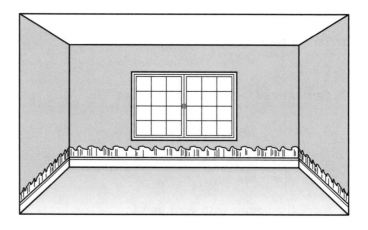

Hang a wall-covering border above the base molding to add dimension.

Extend-a-Window Frame

You could call this idea a window treatment for a window that has little architecture of its own but wants to be the focal point in the room. By framing the window frame in a paper border (especially one with architectural motifs), you give it starring-role status.

To frame a window with wall covering, you'll need to choose a non-directional border. Hang the border right-side up along the top of the window, and then turn it sideways to go around its sides and upside down under the window frame. You'll also need to *miter* the corners (cut at a 45-degree angle) so they'll have a neat look.

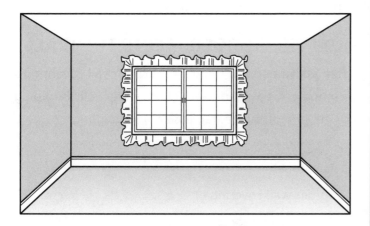

Extend the importance of a window frame with a paper border.

To miter a corner, follow these steps:

1. Hang two strips so they overlap completely at the corner.

2. While the paste is still wet, place a straight edge at a 45-degree angle from the window frame to

the outer corner of the wallpaper frame. Mark the line.

3. Cut along the line with a crafts knife (use the straight edge as a guide) to cut through both layers of paper.

4. Remove the excess scraps and match up the mitered corners with your fingers.

5. Clean up with a sponge.

Once your window frame's in place, you'll notice how that part of your room takes on focal-point status. For months to come, you'll reap the rewards of the afternoon you spent making it happen.

HOW THE BORDER MEETS THE WALL

After you've decided to add a touch of wall covering to your home, it's a clean deal. A little water, a little wiping up—it's one of the neater, easier ways to go.

To hang a wallpaper border, you'll need

- Tape measure
- Border wall covering
- Clean water bucket
- Sharp scissors
- Cellulose sponge

Before you begin, change to comfortable clothes.

1. Measure the section of wall you plan to decorate and cut the border a few inches longer. If you're

QUICK ⬤ PAINLESS

Take care of stubborn edges or corners of wall covering that pop up later by keeping a tube of wall-covering adhesive on hand.

hanging a border at the ceiling, a good place to begin and end the border is in a corner. If you're pasting a border above the base molding, natural stopping points are at doorways.

2. Fill your water bucket with tepid water and set it on the kitchen counter where you can conveniently handle the paper.

3. Loosely roll up the border and lay it in the water.

4. Carefully, draw the border through the water to activate the paste, making sure no spots on the paste side are left dry. Drip the excess water back into the bucket and, without creasing it, gently fold the border back on itself, matching the paste sides together. Allow the paste to set up for about two minutes. Then, pull the layers apart.

5. Position the border on the wall where you want it, leaving a two-inch overhang at the beginning.

6. When you reach a stopping point, crease the border where you plan to cut it with the point of your scissors. Pull the paper away from the wall and cut carefully along the crease line.

7. Re-attach the border to the wall and wipe over it with a damp sponge to remove the excess paste and water.

8. Add more sections, as necessary, being sure to allow for matching the pattern.

YOU'LL THANK YOURSELF LATER

Invest in a comfortable two- or three-step utility stool that you can keep in a closet. It's much easier to handle than a ladder.

Getting Time on Your Side

	The Old Way	The Lazy Way
Painting a wall	3 hours	1 hour
Painting a room	12 hours	3 hours
Wallpapering	Using pre-pasted, old paper you had to trim by hand, endless hours	Using the pre-trimmed wall covering, 1 hour
Wainscoting	Hanging a wainscot, 10 hours	Applying a border, 2–3 hours
Decorating an entire room with wallpaper	20 hours	5 hours

Floor Shows

Nothing puts you more at ease than solid ground beneath your feet. A pleasant texture isn't a bad idea, either, such as the sense of earth you get when you walk on a plush carpet of cool, green grass and the thrill of freedom that seizes your soles on a runway of sun-warmed sand. If only you could take it home....

To some degree, you can.

The purpose of this chapter is to help you put a lazy twist on the way you cover your floors and to become more aware of the surfaces you walk on and how they treat your feet. Then, I show you how to spoil your sensible feet by what you put on your floors in the future. First, let's talk about flooring in general and how to care for the different types.

NO FEET, NO SERVICE

Your existing floors welcome walk-ins, let you step all over them, and endure your scuffs and treads with years of uncomplaining service.

It's my guess that there's little you want to do to change your existing floors. They're either laid with carpet or resilient

flooring, tiled with ceramic or stone, or planked with wood. Unless you want to call in the professionals for a makeover or do a major do-it-yourself project of laying a tongue-and-groove laminate floor over an existing one, you plan to keep up the basic flooring you have.

On the next few pages, you'll find general information about floor-covering and tips on how to maintain it. After that, I get to the lazier stuff.

Carpet Caper

Carpet fibers are usually composed of nylon, polyester, polypropylene, or wool. Synthetic carpets will be tougher and more stain-resistant than wool carpets. You can buy carpeting in three varieties:

- Cut pile: Yarn loops sheared off at the top. More durable cut pile carpets will have a higher number of twists in the carpet yarn.

- Loop pile: A compact weave of uncut yarn loops. To check for durability, push the loops aside to see how densely the tufts are attached to the backing. Density means quality.

- Cut and loop: Sheared and uncut yarn loops combined.

Use soft, thick-cut piles in bedrooms and dining rooms where they won't be worn out quickly. For high-traffic rooms, use a highly twisted pile or dense loop pile.

To care for your carpet, follow these suggestions:

- Blot up spills immediately with a white cloth or paper towels; don't rub and scrub them.

- Apply soap and water or a carpet cleaner. (Be sure to read label instructions.)

- Get your carpets, especially wool ones, professionally cleaned periodically.

Smile! You're on Ceramic Tile

Perfect for bathroom and kitchen floors, the waterproof, stain-resistant floor of ceramic tile is easy to maintain. However, its cold, hard surfaces amplify noise, offer no resilience or comfort while you stand on them, and can be slippery when wet.

To clean ceramic tile, check out these tips:

- Scrub your ceramic floor with soap and water or a non-abrasive household cleaner. No waxing.

- When the grout between the tiles becomes stained from contact with moisture, bleach it with grout bleach and a toothbrush.

- Seal the grout with a latex grout sealer after bleaching it.

Looks Like Laminate Flooring

Laminate flooring, an affordable substitute for natural wood or stone flooring, is mess-free to install and exceptionally easy to maintain. Although it's durable and highly stain-resistant, it can be scratched.

To care for your laminate floor, follow these suggestions:

- Place a doormat inside the door to collect dirt and sand that may scratch the floor.

QUICK PAINLESS

Take the hard, cold, and slip potential of a ceramic bathroom floor out from under your feet with latex-backed, plush-piled, cotton throw rugs.

- Place floor protectors under the furniture legs. If you have furniture on casters, use only clean, seamless plastic caster wheels.

- Vacuum (don't use beater-bar vacuums or electric brooms) as needed or dust mop.

- Spot spray on soiled areas with recommended laminate cleaner. You can also use a blend of vinegar and water solution. (Other cleaners may leave a dull film.) Caution: Steel wool or scouring powders will scratch the floor.

- Wipe up the spot-cleaned areas and damp mop.

- Dry with a rag.

Resilient Flooring

Vinyl floors are comfortable to stand on, and dishes are less likely to break when they fall on them. Resilient flooring is easy to repair and clean and comes in thousands of designs, even some that appear to be stone, wood, or ceramic. Cheapest and least durable? Vinyl composition tiles. Inlaid vinyl is more expensive and longer lasting.

To maintain your resilient floor, follow these tips:

- Vacuum or sweep vinyl to remove debris.

- Mop with a mild household cleaner or soap and water.

The Hard Stuff: Stone, Granite, and Marble

Floors laid with tiles of marble, granite, or slate have some of the same disadvantages of ceramic tile; they're slippery when wet, cold, and non-resilient.

YOU'LL THANK YOURSELF LATER

Place doormats outside your doors and cotton rag rugs on the other side of the threshold to catch dirt and debris. You'll keep the dirt at the door instead of moving it through the house.

On the bright side, they're beautiful and extremely long lasting. You'll want to keep marble out of the kitchen because it's susceptible to acids from spilled juice. Granite shouldn't go there, either, because it takes on stains from grease. Stone floors are perfect for high-traffic entries and living areas where they combine well with soft area rugs and upholstered furniture.

To maintain your stone floor, use these hints:

- Get new floors professionally sealed.
- Clean your stone floor with a mild household cleaner or soap and water. Never use abrasives that will dull and scratch its finish.

Hardwood Floors and Soft Ones, Too

The classic wood floor is loved for its warmth and flexibility. Like a living thing, it shrinks and expands with the seasons and, when sealed with at least two coats of polyurethane, can endure high traffic and gentle cleaning. Because contact with a lot of moisture will cause it to swell, a wood floor is not a good idea for bathrooms. However, it's fine for kitchens and every other room in the house.

Soft wood floors, such as those made from pine, will dent. Eventually, you'll look lovingly at those dented textures and say that your floor has character.

To care for a wood floor, follow these tips:

- Vacuum and mop your wood floor with a mild, non-abrasive cleaner. (Murphy's Oil Soap is a classic.) Never use hot water for scrubbing or pour water directly onto a wood floor.

QUICK PAINLESS

When you lay a sisal area rug or carpet over a hardwood floor, sandwich a rug pad between the two layers to keep the sisal from "sanding down" the wood floor's finish.

- Install felt pads on the bottoms of furniture legs to prevent them from scratching your floor.
- Refinish your wood floor every 15 or 20 years.

RUGS: LAID BACK AND LOVING IT

Ever step out of a warm cocoon of a bed onto a frostbitten floor? Or slip on a slick ceramic floor after a hot shower? Leave a trail of dirt clods behind you after entering the house?

Rugs slip into the picture for the sole purpose of easing your pains and rescuing you from unexpected decorating problems. Here are some ways they serve you best:

- Protect carpet from high-traffic spots.
- Reduce noise levels.
- Soften the hard look and feel of stone or ceramic tile.
- Anchor a sitting group.
- Keep dirt at the door.
- Define several areas in one room.
- Soften the sound as well as the wear and tear on stairway treads.
- Dress up a boring carpet.
- Create instant decorative impact.
- Put texture on a hard-surfaced floor.

Rugs are as ancient as the people who made them. For centuries, they've been braided, twisted, woven, and wound together to soften dirt floors and warm the walls of caves and castles. Now, most rugs are manufactured by computer technology. Still, some cultures remain to offer us the look of handmade beauties we can buy and use at home.

Here's a short list of handmade and manufactured rug types you can buy and tips on how to care for them.

Cut, Loop, and Latex

Constructed loosely like carpeting, pile rugs come in cut, loop, and cut-and-loop piles that are grounded in fabric and treated with a non-slip latex backing. Most care labels will tell you that you can machine wash these rugs in cool water and dry them in low heat.

Rag Rugs

Chindis (Indian rag rugs) and American rag rugs are woven on looms set with sturdy, cotton strings called "warp" threads.

Rag strips (known as weft threads) are woven in and out across the warp threads and pushed snugly together until they form a sturdy, flat-weave rectangular rug. You can wash most American rag rugs in a machine because they'll be colorfast. If you buy an imported rag rug for its beauty, care for it by washing it separately in cold water and a mild detergent because the colors might bleed. Check the care label before purchase if you want to avoid extra work.

Dhurrie Spirit

Evolved from ancient cotton coverings for floors and beds, dhurries are woven by hand in India of cotton, wool, or jute and are noted for their soft colors, intriguing designs,

A COMPLETE WASTE OF TIME

The 3 Worst Things to Do When Caring for Rugs:

1. Wash imported rugs in hot water.

2. Tumble dry rubber-backed rugs at high temperatures.

3. Forget to buy rug pads for non-latex-backed rugs.

IF YOU'RE SO
INCLINED

Save old clothing and chenille bedspreads that can be torn into rag strips for rugs. Give them to someone who weaves rag rugs.

reversibility, and durability. Dhurries are ideal for high traffic areas and places where they can show off their designs. Check the care label before purchasing one. Some can be washed; others must be dry-cleaned. Also, never put a hand-woven rug directly on carpet. To keep the colors from discoloring your carpet, lay a rug pad between the rug and the carpet.

Braided Rugs

Long strips of cotton rags, chenille (silk), or wool are braided—yes, like hair—to make thick strands that are laid next to each other in a circular fashion and stitched together. You can wash cotton braided rugs in a mild detergent and small wool rugs in a soap made especially for wool. Otherwise, treat chenille and wood braided rugs the same way you would treat wall-to-wall carpeting: Vacuum frequently and spot clean.

Oriental Weaves

Ancient cut-pile weaving methods have evolved into machine-made processes that produce look-alike rugs loosely known at your local home store as Oriental weaves. An Oriental weave rug is likely to be the plushest of any rug you select, and you'll value it for its comfort underfoot and for its pattern and coloration. Care for it as you would care for your carpet or follow the instructions that are attached to the rug at the time of purchase. Always slip a rug pad between it and your floor to cushion its pile crush, extend its life, and keep the colors from staining the floor beneath it.

Chain-Stitch Rugs

Colorful wool or cotton yarns chain-stitched in delicate rows over the entire surface of a cotton canvas create a picture rug. Check the label for care instructions.

Natural Floor Coverings

Eco-friendly, breathe-easy, wholly natural rug products hold strong appeal for *Lazy Way* homeowners. With a sisal carpet here and a straw mat there, you can bring that outdoorsy feeling inside or take these rugs outdoors under cover for living al fresco. Here's a list of plant-life rug products you can buy:

- Sisal: The Mexican agave plant strands are turned into durable, well-tailored rugs and wall-to-wall carpeting. Their tight weaves are handsome, rarely come undone, and are stimulating underfoot.

- Coir: The golden-brown husk of the coconut palm is more roughly textured than sisal but is less expensive and more durable. Coir rugs turn up most often on doorsteps where they politely let you wipe your shoes on them.

- Raffia: Phillipine grass is woven into lightweight mats that will break down under wet conditions.

- Rush, sea grass, and rice straw: The soft, loose textures of these plant materials are woven into practical and attractive mats that are assembled into larger rugs and carpeting. To prevent their breakdown and prolong their life, keep these rugs under cover and away from water.

YOU'LL THANK YOURSELF LATER

Visit home stores and import stores to acquaint yourself with the inventory of rugs available to you. Read their labels and check their prices for future reference.

■ Jute: A strong fiber from East Indian plants is turned into cording and woven into burlap bags and firm foundations for rug making.

On the previous pages, I've mentioned the use of rug pads and rug grips a number of times. When you shop for rugs, keep them in mind, especially if you purchase a rug without a rubber or latex backing.

Here's what a rug pad can do for you:

■ Give your rug a non-slip grip on the floor.

■ Allow ventilation for vacuuming and moisture evaporation if it has an open weave.

■ Cushion and prevent the pile crush of the rug it supports.

■ Extend the life of the rug by keeping its back from breaking down underfoot.

■ Keep the rug from discoloring the floor it lies upon.

Most rug pads are made from a lightweight, rubbery foam that you can cut with a scissors to fit your rug. They'll wash in warm, soapy water. Some rug pads have an adhesive on one side so they'll stick to small rugs and stay in place.

DIAL ONE: AREA RUGS TO THE RESCUE

After you've laid down small rugs to alleviate the practical problems of dirt-tracking, slipping, and other things that make the feet in your house uncomfortable, you can entertain the idea of laying down a rug or two to solve

QUICK ◎ PAINLESS

Is the oil from your feet matting down the carpet beside your bed? Slip in a velvety, foot-welcoming bedside rug to put an end to the problem.

aesthetic problems. That means you can look at rugs for more than just practical reasons. You can choose them for their beauty, their colors, and the sense of style they'll bring to a room. First, you need to know that when you look for a decorative rug, you'll find most of them in these sizes:

- 4' × 6'
- 6' × 8'
- 8' × 10'

Here's a list of rug uses for each size:

- Four-by-six-foot rugs work well in entry halls, at the bottom of stairs, and at door openings. They smooth the transitions from outdoors to inside, from room to room, and from one floor to another.

- Six-by-eight-foot rugs are the best size for creating a small conversation group and being the center of attraction. Upholstered chairs can wrap comfortably around its edges, and a coffee table in the center will further anchor it.

- Eight-by-ten-foot rugs are suitable for conversation anchors in large rooms or as a near wall-to-wall carpet in a small room. Very large rooms can use two or three of these rugs to define two or three conversation groups.

Here are a couple of room scenes you can create with area rugs of various sizes.

IF YOU'RE SO
INCLINED

Consider a large area rug to anchor your dining room table and chairs. It'll quiet the room if the floor is stone or hardwood and keep the chairs from scratching the floor.

Spice from the Orient

When you have a boring carpet and a lot of crushed pile around the chairs in a conversation area, spice it up with a new and beautiful conversation-starting area rug. It can be an antique Persian rug you've picked up at an estate sale or something new you've purchased from a home store.

You'll need

Room with a boring carpet and worn-down conversation area

Rug pad to fit the area rug

Oriental weave area rug to suit the size of your room (8' × 10' rugs are a good size for a conversation area) and coordinate with the color of the carpet

Scissors

1 Move the furniture back from the center of the room.

2 If necessary, trim the rug pad with your scissors to fit the area rug.

3 Lay the rug pad in the center of the room so that the margins of carpet around it are as equal as you can make them.

4 Lay the area rug over the rug pad.

5 Arrange the furniture around and on the area rug, anchoring the furniture legs on it for an intimate grouping.

QUICK ⬤ PAINLESS

Don't be shy about bringing your sofas and chairs onto the area rug. Avoid the doctor's waiting-room look you'll get by lining up your seating pieces around the room.

When Bigger Is Better

Let's say that the problem you have is a small area rug—a 4' × 6' with a gorgeous design you want to show off. Its drawback is its size: It's too small for the conversation area you'd like to put it in. Here's how you can put it where you want it without its small size looking out of proportion with the rest of the room.

You'll need

Hardwood floor or a low-pile, plain carpeted floor in a living room or family room where you have a seating group around a coffee table

6' × 8' rug pad

6' × 8' rice straw mat or sisal rug

4' × 6' decorative area rug

1 Move the furniture back to the wall out of the way.

2 Lay the 6' × 8' rug pad at the center of the conversation area, leaving even borders of hardwood or carpeted flooring around it.

3 Lay the 6' × 8' sisal or straw mat rug over the rug pad.

4 Center the 4' × 6' decorative rug on the 6' × 8' rug.

5 Arrange the furniture on and around the rugs.

6 You've made a balanced focal point out of your small rug by giving it a "frame" or border of natural material. The sisal or straw rug gives you a good transition to the floor covering beneath the conversation group.

IF YOU'RE SO INCLINED

Try the project called **When Bigger Is Better** one size up. Center a 6' × 8' decorative rug on an 8' × 10' sisal or straw mat in a room that is large enough to handle the larger rug sizes.

Easy Runner

Sometimes, rugs are so beautiful that you hate to tread on them. When this happens and you discover a runner that fits beautifully with your dinnerware, bring it home for service on your dining room table. Its life will be easy and frivolous, completely decorative.

You'll need

A rectangular dining room table

A three-foot-wide woven runner three feet longer than the length of your table

1 Clear the table.

2 Lay the runner over the length of the table, centering it in the middle of the table.

3 Check that the "drops" (lengths hanging over the ends of the table) are equal and not in the laps of diners.

4 Furnish diners with colorful napkins that match the colors in the rag-rug runner.

Dining has never been more comfortable or casual.

Getting Time on Your Side

	The Old Way	**The Lazy Way**
Cleaning a floor	Scratching it with abrasives	Keeping it like new with gentle cleaning
Cleaning a carpet	Steam-cleaning it every year and wearing off the finish	Spot-cleaning and rare professional cleanings
Washing rugs	Bleeding rug colors into your laundry	Reading care labels
Putting a rug down	Discoloring your floor or carpet	Using a rug pad
Choosing a decorative area rug	Catch-as-catch can	Surefire hits
Arranging a conversation area around a rug	Over time	An afternoon

Chapter
eight

Effortless Window Dressing

You don't have to apologize if your windows aren't "properly" covered. Remember the "right stuff" 80s and the push for "my kind of stuff" in the 90s? Hey, it's the new millenium—time for breaking out of that intimidation box and cutting through to what you really want—getting on with your life.

Window dressings, like fashion, are lightening up and becoming less work to assemble. We're dressing our windows in casual, carefree fabrics that simply let in the light; they don't scream for attention or cost an arm and a leg.

Is it any wonder? Who has time for all that drama and expense? Complicated is out, simple is in, and you're in luck. You can do the window thing the "lazy-stuff" way and still be in step with the times.

WELCOME TO WINDOWS

Your windows are your eyes to the world. They

- Let in the light (and sometimes fresh air).
- Give you a view of the neighborhood.
- Tell you what the weather is like.

You love your windows, every precious inch of them (you wish they were bigger), but when you've had enough of the light and the view, you're glad you can pull down the shades and settle into your soft, inside world.

Like people, windows come in all sizes—tiny side-lights in doorways, modest three- to four-foot-wide double-hungs, slender casements that open outward, and paneful affairs that wrap around a room and reach from floor to ceiling. Like people, they make certain demands about what they wear.

Some windows beg to go without curtains because they're spectacular just the way they are and no one in the house sees a need to cover them. People walk by and say they're works of art.

Other windows are better when they're dressed a bit. Privacy is one good reason; light control, a second. Another is that curtains help blend windows into an interior's decor, softening their hard edges with fabrics.

YOU'LL THANK YOURSELF LATER

Acquaint yourself with window terms so you can speak windowese with a store clerk and interpret package instructions when you shop for easy window stuff.

Window Wear

What we moderns use to dress our windows (called a window treatment) falls into two basic categories:

- A shade or blind for light control and privacy
- A decorative fabric panel hung on a curtain rod

Your window treatment can consist of either element alone or a combination of both. That seems simple enough; doesn't it? It's not. Between these two principal approaches lie a profusion (and confusion) of commercial products and style choices, giving you myriad ways to dress your windows.

When you're a lazy junkie, you keep your priorities straight and don't let the crowded shelves intimidate you. I'll give you a run-through of things you should know before you head out to the well-stocked world of window fashions. For example, did you know that "return" isn't just another word for taking something back to the store?

What's in a Frame?

You don't have to take a class in windows (that's not computer talk) to know what you need to dress them. Just a few simple word definitions ought to do it. We could start with its frame.

When you uncover a window, you find a framed panel of glass. You'll see that it's been jammed (on a *jamb*) into a hole cut in the wall, which gives it a certain depth. The depth of the jamb gives you a place for an inside-mounted window treatment.

IF YOU'RE SO INCLINED

Take an inventory of the windows in your living quarters. Write down your intentions for changing their looks. It can't hurt to make a plan.

At the bottom of the window is a perch or window *sill*. To cover the raw edges and gaps of the jammed-in window during construction, carpenters installed a frame (also called a *casing*) around the window opening on the face of the wall. It's usually a pretty molding with a bend and a curve that goes with the rest of the architecture of the room. The expression *return* on a window means the depth or thickness of the casing as it returns to the wall or to the jamb.

Windows in the buff are meant to be beautiful as well as functional. Check out the diagram for a clearer picture of a window's parts.

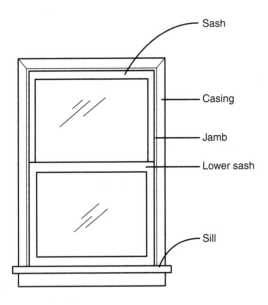

Parts of a window frame.

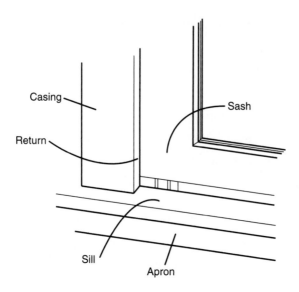

The lower section of a window.

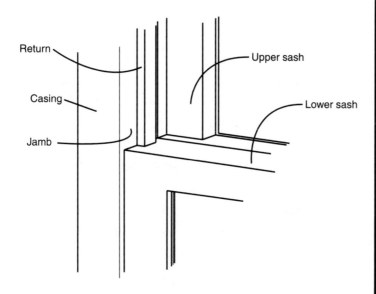

The upper section of a window.

Take a discovery trip while you're rambling about. Check out an import store or a specialty home store to see more unusual window fashion possibilities.

Where Window and Treatment Meet

When you plan a window treatment, you need to know how to measure your window so that everything works out when you get the treatment home from the store. If you know a few simple words, we can talk windows with ease for the rest of this chapter.

Basically, window treatments are mounted in one of two ways:

On the *inside* of a window frame or window casing

On the *outside* of a window opening on the window frame itself or on the wall around or above it

FROM BARE TO DRESSED-TO-THE-NINES

You probably have a combination of needs when it comes to covering your windows. You can have all of them met by mixing and matching these excellent hassle-free choices.

Undressed

The more public rooms of your home hold the perfect windows for the now popular unadorned look. Living rooms, dining rooms, family rooms, and kitchens all present opportunities to regard their windows as architectural gems or grand openings to the light. Leaving them as is is as lazy as redecorating gets.

Barely Dressed

Thinly clad windows are covered only by shades and blinds. The intention of the window covering is privacy and light control. You can buy shades and blinds in a wide array of vinyl, wood, metal, paper, and fabric. They come pleated, double-pleated, and slatted. Some hang simply by hooks. Others hang from brackets that are set into or on the frame of the window. Shades and blinds are often considered the undergarments of window dressing. I disagree. These days, some of them are so beautiful that it's a shame to hide them under thick, decorative layers that take up a lot of space.

Dressier

Sheers are classic, readymade panels of thin, almost transparent fabrics that fold and gather gracefully on a rod. They've looked great for decades and continue to be the first choice for gracing a simple window. You can use sheers as:

- A privacy panel that lets in the light while it hides the view of the interior in its folds

- A pretty overlay to hide a rather ordinary shade

- Sheer room-decorating elegance that blends easily into most interiors

Sheers have a lot of relatives: Fine laces and embroidered voiles, some with lightly printed patterns on filmy fabrics. They come in a variety of long-length, mid-size, and half curtains for windows of all sizes. You can top off your windows with a variety of traditional valances and smart, new scarves that you drape over swag hooks.

QUICK ●⊞● PAINLESS

A mini dress-up idea for a bare double-hung window: Set glass plates with hobnail or etched designs on the window sash (ledge) at the center of the window.

All Dressed Up

Textured and printed fabric panels play the dressed-up roles in carefree, lazy-style window dressing. Often, these decorative fabric panels don't cover the entire window but are used economically as side panels to frame privacy sheers underneath. You can buy decorative panels three ways:

- Readymade with rod-pockets for hanging on rods that are hidden inside the curtain.
- Readymade tab-tops for hanging on decorative rods.
- Custom order for fussy windows. When you can't find what you want on the racks, you might need to order window coverings through interior design stores. Be sure to get an estimate before you commit because this can turn into a costly venture.

BARE IS BEAUTIFUL

How many of your windows can you leave undressed? This not-so-revolutionary idea will save you hours of your precious time. Bare windows require no planning, no shopping, no style choices, and no need to get out the screwdriver. Where is it written that you *must* cover all your windows?

Most of the windows in my house go fully exposed to natural views and gorgeous sunlight. No, I don't live in some idyllic place in the country with horses grazing on green hills. I'm smack in the middle of suburbia in a goofy little post-war 60s ranch house. In spite of all the dense housing around me, I'm convinced that many of

my windows (and the light they bring into the house) do not deserve to be covered with dust-gathering fabrics. Nor do I want to be disconnected from the natural world around me, even at night.

When you remove old curtains, you can count the benefits of bare:

- You'll reclaim the space the curtains took up.
- Your windows get a chance to boast their architecture.
- The sunshine inside the house is more abundant.
- The view is good, if not beautiful.
- You can keep an eye on the kids and neighborhood dogs.
- You'll know when the garbage man comes.
- The health nuts you see jogging by will inspire (or depress) you.
- Your plants will love it.

The perfect time to try the bare look in a non-private room in the house is between treatments. Strip away the dusty old trappings of the past window dressing and live for a while with your window in its bare simplicity. Then, decide whether it's worth putting energy and expense into a new window treatment.

PRIVACY, PLEASE

When you need a little light control for sleeping and a whole lot of privacy for bathing and other things you'd like to do unseen, there are two easy options for keeping out what you don't want coming in.

The 3 Worst Things to Do When Shopping for a Shade:

1. Forget to measure the window before you leave home.

2. Ignore the package instructions.

3. Be afraid to ask for help.

You've Got It Made with a Shade

If privacy is your thing and you want to achieve it simply and instantly, hang a rice paper shade. You can buy roll-ups in paper, fabric, wood, and vinyl. The wood and vinyl ones you find in home improvement centers and housewares departments are decidedly popular, sturdy, and easy to clean. I prefer the rice paper and matchstick blinds from import stores for their ephemeral beauty, even though you can't wash them, and they age in humid conditions so I know that I'll have to replace them in three or four years.

Installing roll-ups couldn't be easier. Two triangular hanging loops embedded in a simple, lightweight head rail at the top of the shade hold the hooks of the roll-up (included in the package). It'll take you about 10 minutes to hang a roll-up.

First, you have to determine what size shade to buy. If you intend to install just the shade without an overlay of fabric, and you have no concerns about marring the window frame, it will work best if the shade overlaps the window opening by two inches on each side. Lengths are predetermined by the manufacturer.

If you don't want to damage the window frame, choose a shade that's the same width as the outside measurement of the frame. Plan to install the hooks at the point where the top of the window frame meets the wall; no one ever sees what goes on up there.

What you'll need

- Shade of the correct size to fit the location you've chosen (with mounting hooks)
- Hammer
- Small nail
- Pliers
- Pencil
- Tape measure
- Step stool
- Phillips screwdriver

Unfold your step stool in front of the window before you begin.

1. Unroll the shade to check its condition.

2. Re-roll to make it easier to handle.

3. Hold the shade up to the window frame to mark the places where you'll mount the hooks. If you're mounting them on the window frame, locate them so that the head rail at the top of the shade falls parallel with the window's inside casing.

4. Center the shade on the window from side to side, and put your pencil through the shade loops to mark the site for the hooks. Use a measuring tape to make sure the marks are at the same height (if on the window frame) or depth (if on the top of the frame).

Whenever you come to the end of a room-changing project, invite friends over. It'll give you time to sit back and bask in the glow of their compliments.

The Lazy Way

5. You probably won't be able to screw the hooks into the frame without "starting" the holes. If you have a drill or driver, you can use it to drill tiny holes. Just as easy: Start the hole with a hammer and nail by tapping the nail in a quarter of an inch (just enough to give the screw end of the hook a start) and then removing it.

6. Screw in the hooks tentatively and do a final check of their placement by gently placing the shade loops on them.

7. Screw the hooks in securely, turning them with your fingers at first. When they stiffen under your hand, tighten them some more with pliers.

8. Hang the shade and unroll, pulling the cording evenly around it.

9. Attach the cord holder to the side of the window frame with the Phillips screwdriver. Roll up the shade to the desired height, secure, and enjoy your privacy.

Flying Blind

Manufacturers make it easy to hang classic mini and Venetian blinds, and home centers make it easy to shop for them. They're loaded with wood and vinyl blinds of all colors and flavors.

The main reasons for choosing blinds over roll-up shades are durability and light control. Durability varies from brand to brand, of course, but I'd give blinds a longer life span than shades. They're bigger dust-gatherers than shades but durable enough to clean with a damp cloth. Blinds let light slip through their slats without changing their position on the window. You can control the amount of light that comes through the spaces between the slats with a "wand" at the side of the blind. Blinds hang by brackets that can be mounted inside the window frame (inside mount) or on the outside of the frame (outside mount). They take a little more time to mount than a roll-up shade (about 10 minutes more).

First, decide whether you want to hang your blind inside the window casing or outside on the frame, and make your measurements accordingly. Personally, I like the inside mount for a sleek, smooth look. If the return on your window doesn't give you space for an inside mount, an outside mount is your only choice.

Buy the kit kind that includes everything you need except a tape measure and a screwdriver. Check the back of the package for the instructions. If you can't see and decipher the instructions at the time of purchase, don't buy, or you could get home and discover that they're in another language.

What you'll need:

- Blind kit in measurements to fit your window (hardware included)
- Tape measure
- Pencil
- Electric drill kit
- Screwdriver

YOU'LL THANK YOURSELF LATER

If you don't want to spend money on expensive power tools, borrow them from friends or check the Yellow Pages for rental sources.

Read the blind instructions and then follow these steps:

1. Unwrap the blind kit.

2. Review the instructions.

3. Center the blind on the part of the window frame where you plan to hang it.

4. Make tentative marks with a pencil for the placement of the brackets. Put your pencil through the pre-drilled screw holes in the brackets and mark the spots.

5. Check your placement of the marks with a tape measure.

6. Pre-drill the screw holes with your drill.

7. Working one bracket and screw at a time, drive the screws through the brackets into the window frame, but don't secure them yet.

8. Check the fit of the blind's head rail between the brackets. If it all checks out, finish tightening the screws.

9. Return the head rail to the brackets.

10. Slide on the decorative blind valance that came with the kit.

11. Release the blind and tighten the cords.

QUICK  *PAINLESS*

Instead of spending the time hanging a shade or blind, for a privacy panel, hang sheers on a round tension rod. It's much faster.

PRIVATE, PLUS

When the less-is-more philosophy of dressing a window with a simple (but elegant) blind or shade doesn't satisfy your redecorating palette, add a little something extra to the scene. Think sheers—sheer magic, sheer elegance, added sheer. Nothing big, dark, and dramatic here. Remember, we're going *The Lazy Way*.

Another sure-fire option is lace. You can have it abundantly in inexpensive, washable white and creamy tones, fine weaves, and not-so-fine weaves.

You'll need to fit your rod choice to the panel that piques your decorating desires. Usually sheers and not-so-sheer lace curtains carry rod pockets on the reverse sides of their panels. You just need to thread a tension rod or a bracketed rod through the pockets and fasten them to the window frame.

For big and tall windows, select sheers. You'll get more for your money, and the variety of sheer ready-made panels is notable. The big bonus? Sheer washability. Beyond that, the transparent good looks that these wispy fabrics bring to your light-loving rooms has no end of decorative dividends.

Sheer Magic

Check the decorating sections of department, discount, and specialty stores for pretty sheers to hang on the return inside your window frame. This treatment creates both privacy and good looks.

IF YOU'RE SO
INCLINED

Buy six yards of a colorful sheer fabric from a fabric store. Loop the length over a tension rod set inside the window frame, arrange the gathers, and let the ends "pool" onto the floor. Tuck the raw edges under the pooling.

New versions on the window-treatment horizon are turning sheers into the up-and-coming window fabric of the year. Some are thin voiles with delicate patterns printed on them. Others carry a single motif embroidered into the fabric every 10 inches or so. Look for the new white sheers with stars and flower motifs subtly surfing their fine nets.

For starters, choose the simplest way to hang a pair of sheers—a tension rod. Then, measure the length of your window where the panels will hang. Purchase the rod and sheers and hang them according to package instructions.

Amazing Lace

You don't have to limit your window-dressing options to fabric panels made especially for curtains. You can have fun with easy round tension rods and crocheted tablecloths, the kind you find in stores that specialize in lace curtains and related lace.

My lazy neighbor showed me her lazy-stuff windows the other day. I'm passing her idea on to you. Instead of traveling a long distance to buy readymade curtain panels, she bought four loosely crocheted tablecloths on her way home from work. She threaded a round tension rod through large openings in the weave along one edge of each tablecloth. Then, she mounted the rods inside her window frame at a position that allowed the bottoms of the tablecloths to skirt the windowsill. This left a third of her window panels uncovered at the top. No one could see into the house above that point and she was glad for the extra light that came into the room.

QUICK **PAINLESS**

For ease in calculating the best fullness for your curtains, multiply the width of the window opening by $2^1/_2$.

You can create this window treatment in a tall, narrow window that measures about 72 inches high and 36 inches wide. You'll need a tension rod and two 48-inch-square crocheted tablecloths with a large, heavy pattern. Before you buy, check for large holes in the crocheted pattern along the perimeter of the cloth. Be sure they are big enough for a round tension rod.

Adjust the length of the rod to fit inside the window frame. Push the rod through the wide holes in the perimeter of the tablecloth. Ideally, the holes would be about six inches apart. Insert the rod in the window frame and adjust the folds of the tablecloth fabric on the rod, balancing them across the face of the window.

PRETTIER, PLEASE

At this point in window-making history, tab-tops are consumer favorites in window wear. What's a tab-top? It's the curtain panel with wide, flat loops at the top for hanging it on a decorative rod. If you're already familiar with the tab-top, you're well into lazy redecorating—you and millions of other smart people.

Tab-top panels come in so many different fabrics, it makes your head spin. That's the difficult part—choosing which one. In my opinion, the most graceful tab-top curtains are the sheer, thin Indian cottons, but you might like the no-iron textures of gauze, sleek silks, and polyester fibers. The velvets and graceful satins take a little ironing or steaming to remove creases from readymade packaging.

YOU'LL THANK YOURSELF LATER

Avoid ironing the creased curtain panels you've just pulled out of the package by hanging them on a rod in the bathroom while you take a hot shower. The steam will relax the creases.

Add curve to your tab-top's straight look. Draw a sturdy thread through the hem's outside corner. Pull the panel up to and around the rod, and tie off the thread. Arrange the fabric folds. It might help to look at the example in the photograph section of this book.

How to hang a tab-top curtain: What could be easier? Slip them onto the rod, return the rod to the brackets, arrange the spaces between the tabs on the rod, and walk away. Two minutes of your precious time exchanged for softness, grace, and peace of mind.

SHORT TAKES: SMALL CURTAINS THAT THINK BIG

Give scraps of prehemmed fabrics, such as napkins, kitchen towels, or scarves a surprising, larger purpose: Decorating a window. Take advantage of fringed pieces that add style and a touch of class to your place.

Napkin Toss

Small windows are usually treated with readymade, rod-pocketed cafe curtains you can buy, but sometimes, you just don't want to shop for one more thing. This mini-curtain is not exactly a normal, run-of-the-mill idea, but it can be assembled in about a minute if you have an attractive napkin in your kitchen drawer and a whim to try something new and quick. This treatment is useful in a small kitchen window where privacy is not a factor.

You'll need a large dinner napkin and a tension rod (the extra one you stashed in your decorating closet). Follow the package instructions to hang the rod. Then, hang the napkin "curtain" over the tension rod, just off center. Pull one corner of the napkin lower than another for a casual, laid-back look. Check the photograph section of this book for an example.

Pin-Up Panel

You've fallen into the decorating trap—that place where you think you actually *like* decorating. This project is only for victims of the decorating trap who want a special touch at the top of a boring privacy panel. Such things are called *toppers,* and if you do a lazy-style topper, you want something that isn't going to cost you more than five minutes of your time to hang or any time spent thinking about how to do it.

You'll need two tacks and an antique runner or velvet scarf. To see if this idea works for you, start out with two thumb tacks to push through the fabric onto the window frame over the privacy panel. Center the length of the panel across the top of the window, planning your tack attack so the fabric will span the window gracefully and its ends will fall gently down the side of the window frame. Tack up the fabric and stand back to see whether you like the look. Make any adjustments you feel are necessary.

If you do like it, check drapery trim sections for a couple of decorative drapery pins to replace the tacky tacks. You can also super-glue antique buttons onto the heads of your tacks.

RODS THAT ROLL IN A HURRY

The range of curtain rods available is astonishing if you categorize them according to style. Don't even try. It's too much work. For lazy purposes, you need to know

Cut yourself a decorating break by browsing through inspirational books in a bookstore. Buy yourself a cup of Sky Between the Branches tea or a latte to sip while you turn the pages of your best pick. See if it's wonderful enough to add to your home library.

Buy prepackaged kits complete with a rod, brackets, and decorative finials. It's one-stop shopping at its finest.

only one thing about rods: How they function. You can put the whole lot of them into just two categories:

- Tension rods are fitted with inner springs that push the ends of the rod out against the inside casing of the window, holding it securely in place.

- Bracketed rods have bent elbows at the ends to attach to hardware on the face of the window

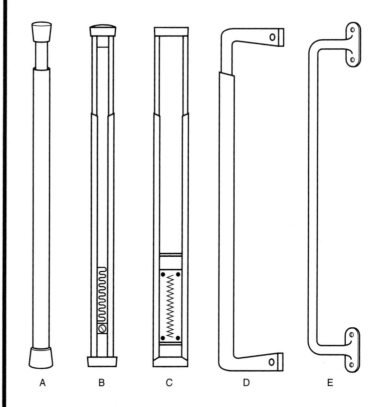

A. Round tension rod
B. Oval tension rod (back view)
C. Continental tension rod (back view)
D. Metal rod-pocket rod with separate bracket hardware
E. Decorative rod with built-in bracket

Types of curtain rods.

frame or on the wall beside or above the window. Some brackets are separate from the rod; others are part of it. Some bracketed rods are bold, decorative parts of the window treatment, whereas others hide inside the folds of the curtain.

If you know how a rod functions on your particular window, you can make the style choice accordingly when you purchase it.

Ease-the-Tension Rods

Tension rods are the busy person's answer to window pains. They've been around for decades, but they just don't get any better when it comes to Jack-Be-Quick. You can take yours round, oval, or continental (a bar that's 2 1/2 inches wide). All three are mounted *inside* the window casing, not *on* the window frame. For the round and oval tension rods, you need curtains with one-inch-wide rod pockets. The continental requires rod pockets that are at least three inches wide. To hang them, follow the instructions that come with the package.

Rods with Style and Stretch

Curtain rods think they're house jewelry. Time was when rods were limited to sliding secretly through rod pockets stitched into the backs of fabric panels. With the arrival of tab-top curtains, rods have come out of the closet wearing smart, new finishes and fancy *finials*. You can still buy the metal kind that hide behind curtains (they're in the section with the tension rods), but check out the current ones while you're on the move. Read the instructions for hanging them before you get them home.

Hanging a panel of curtains calls for a sit-back-and-gaze session. Treat yourself to something—food, music, a latte—while you appreciate your new decorating accomplishment.

The Lazy Way

Getting Time on Your Side

	The Old Way	**The Lazy Way**
Hanging a shade	30 minutes	10 minutes
Hanging a bracketed rod	20 minutes	10 minutes
Shopping for curtains trips	2 trips (one without a measuring tape)	1 trip
Choosing a shade	Trips to three stores	1 store will do it
Pressing curtains	2 hours	Nada

Flick-of-Wrist Lighting

Call me lazy—another word for quick-witted. Smart enough to know you don't need a degree in lighting design to pull off a well lit home. A few tricks up your sleeve, and you'll cover the subject in less time than it takes to light a fire in the hearth.

You're probably one of the lucky ones. Builders of your home took care of the basics of built-in lighting for you. You already have the necessities of general lighting—overhead chandeliers and recessed wall washers, a track light or two. All you have to do to get comfortably lit is add a floor lamp here, a table lamp there, and some kind of mood light that will set your pulse up a notch.

Maybe you weren't so lucky. When you first chose your living quarters, you did so in the daylight and didn't think to ask about lighting. The night you moved in, you reached for the light switch by the door and your magic touch was gone. You stumbled around in the dark until you could dig a lamp out of a carton and light your way inside.

WHEN THE SUN GOES DOWN

Your life has no light in it after dark unless you have a lighting plan. There are three parts to the plan for lighting up your nights:

- General
- Task
- Accent

Hold that thought. I get back to it in 20 seconds.

THANK YOU, MR. EDISON

Electric lights come to you courtesy of Thomas Edison and his successors who manufacture light sources of all shapes and sizes. When you go to a lighting store or home improvement center, don't be overwhelmed by the dazzling firmament of lights that beam down on you; you can knock the whole lot of them down to three basic types:

- Portable free-standing plug-in lamps (floor lamps, table lamps, can lights, picture lights, strip lights, and pendants hung on ceiling hooks)
- Ceiling fixtures (pendants, chandeliers, down lights, recessed spotlights, and track lighting)
- Wall-mounted fixtures (sconces, strip lights, and picture lights)

You can use many of these light sources to light a whole room, accent a special place, or perform a task. You'll need some combination of general, task, and accent lights in every room in your house.

A COMPLETE WASTE OF TIME

The 3 Worst Things to Do When Buying a Light Fixture:

1. Buy something you can't legally electrify yourself.

2. Buy track heads that aren't compatible with your tracks; know your track brand.

3. Buy an awkwardly sized shade for a lamp.

IT'S IN THE SWITCH

General lighting is the fundamental illumination that fills a room. If you're a morning riser, you wake up to the least expensive light source available—the natural ambience of daylight. When the sun slips away, you replace it with switch-on lights that prevent evening shadows from pervading your space.

Ceiling fixtures make up a large portion of general lighting sources for homes. Older versions are typically nothing more than a single glaring light bulb, softened by a glass covering, at the center of the ceiling. Modern houses have a more stylish mix of lighting fixtures that put out varied forms of light.

Recessed spotlights spread light evenly and softly around an entire room, whereas chandeliers insist on being its star attraction. Pendant lamps are smart choices over tables, and track lights can do all sorts of things: Wash a whole wall, spotlight one area of the room, and change a room's mood with the help of a dimmer. Floor lamps and table lamps are general light sources you can just plug in. You can also change the function of the track lights from general use to accenting of a special area of the room.

Connections R Generally EZ

Most of your general lighting needs are resolved by ceiling fixtures set into your home by builders and electricians you've never met. But if your home has a switch by the door that connects to a socket in the room, you have to provide your own general lighting device.

QUICK ◉ *PAINLESS*

When you buy a lamp, take a moment to be sure it is UL (Underwriters Laboratories) approved.

Determine the function of the lamp before you buy the shade. A translucent shade adds to general light levels. An opaque shade directs light downward for reading and similar activities.

That's easy enough. Plugging in a lamp isn't going to take you more than a second. It's mostly a matter of deciding which lamp and shade to buy and where to put it. Here are three general-lighting options to consider:

- A standard floor lamp with a shade will direct the light downward. Place it beside or behind the main piece of furniture in the room. A not-so-standard floor lamp might be a "feather" lamp, a slender, stylish (and expensive) floor lamp that burns a halogen bulb. (I talk light bulbs at the end of the chapter.)

- A *torchere* is a freestanding torch-like light that directs light upward. It's an especially good choice for getting rid of the cavern look of cathedral ceilings.

- A large table lamp with a three-way switch can provide both general lighting and light for such things as reading if you place it on a table near a chair.

Getting on Track

Track heads give you a lot of flexibility in lighting because you can move them, change their style, and change them from track to track in a snap—snap-in, that is. They come in a variety of contemporary styles, and the smaller they are, the more chic (and expensive). If you go to a home improvement center, you can get track heads for $10. Pendant versions (track heads on wires that hang down from the track at any length you choose) will cost upwards of $50 each.

To snap in a track head, you'll need

- Track set in the ceiling by an electrician
- Track heads compatible with your track
- The snap-in instructions that come with the heads

NO-WORK TASK LIGHTING

Task lighting is the nitty-gritty, workaholic lighting you place at your fingertips. It sheds light on your reading, cooking, hobbies, games, bath, and desktop. It gives you the information you need to go down a long, dark hallway. Portable lamps, strip lights, recessed lights, and pendant lamps can be hard workers if you put them in the right locations.

Easy Reader

Instead of spending an hour trying to place your reading lamp in the right position, do it *The Lazy Way*. Sit down in the spot where you'll be doing your reading, and make sure the bottom of the shade falls slightly below eye level (which amounts to about 40–42 inches off the floor). If you'll be using a floor lamp that's also used for general light, it should be about 10 inches behind your shoulder.

Quick Strip

Low-profile strip lights are inexpensive, easily tuck into tight spaces, and plug into existing outlets. That makes them a good choice for under-cabinet lighting where you cook or pay bills. Strip lights are also good as accent shelf lighting in china cupboards and on overhead ledges.

QUICK ⟨•⟩ PAINLESS

When you use track lighting to accent wall objects, aim the fixtures at a 30-degree angle.

Buy the kind that mounts with self-stick adhesive. (Look Ma, no tools.) Foam tape is enclosed separately so you can choose which side of the light channel you'll mount it on (depending upon the direction in which you want the light to shine). Peel off one side of the liner and press it onto the top or one of the sides of the channel. Then, remove the other liner and just press the light bar to the location of your choice. It doesn't get much lazier than that.

ACCENTUATE YOUR POSITIVES

Accent lights focus on visual elements of interest, such as your prized collection of paintings, houseplants, model ships, or other objects of your heart's affections. They put decorative style into redecorating and focal points in your rooms.

Spotlights set into track and recessed lighting are the most common forms of accent lighting, but you need an electrician to install tracks for you. If you already have tracks, it's easy to direct the track lights toward a part of the room you'd like to accent. It's just a matter of directing the lamp in a more downward position to concentrate more light on whatever special object you'd like to illuminate.

If you don't have tracks and you want to assemble a few accent light sources on your own, you can get a lot of look with portable lights that will be less expensive than track lights. They come in the shape of sconces, picture lights, can lights, and even miniature Christmas tree lights. Try them; you'll like them. For little effort, you'll be rewarded with a big chunk of satisfaction. That's a lazy-style promise.

Sconce It

Sconces are usually electrified wall fixtures that an electrician puts in. They're great for entries and hallways because they direct you through the dark in much the same way as ancient wall-hung torches in castle corridors.

We've come a long way down the castle corridors into the light. For modern-day torches, you can hang elegant candle-burning sconces on the wall of a space you'd like to accent—a fireplace mantel, an entry, a mirror. Two sconces are better than one. They make a perfect frame for highlighting the area.

Picture This

Little bands of light in a metal strip are the traditional way to accent your special art pieces. They're portable light fixtures that can go wherever your paintings and posters go.

You can buy picture lights with instructions for hanging at home centers, lighting stores, and home stores with lighting sections. Some picture lights are made with small pinch-on clamps that you simply clip to the picture frame. This type of picture light gives you flexibility and changeability. You can move them from one picture to another as your whims change—no hassle. Other picture lights come with instructions and hardware for screwing the picture lights permanently through the picture frame. Check the package to be sure you're choosing the easier clamp-on type of picture light.

YOU'LL THANK YOURSELF LATER

Don't waste time looking in stores that sell candle-burning sconces if you're looking for the electrically lit kind. Check decorator catalogs and specialty home stores.

Experiment with your clamp-on picture lights. Instead of attaching them to the *top* of the frame (the usual place), attach them to the *bottom* of the frame to shine the light upward on the painting or poster you're highlighting.

Cans That Can

Would you believe a light bulb set into the bottom of a can, shining its beacon upward? The concept is so simple that you can't believe it's real. A cord comes out of the side of the can so you can plug it in to a light socket. It makes perfect sense. Some can lights (for a trifle more money) come on swivels so you can direct them to either side as well as the standard "up" direction of the non-swiveled can light.

Here are some ideas for can lights:

- Put a can light under a plant to create dramatic shadows on the wall.

- Direct several can lights upward to visually open a high ceiling. It's conceivable that you can create a room's whole lighting plan from nothing but can lights—that is, if you don't plan to read, pay bills, or play card games there.

- Create a mood of low-key mystery by placing a can light under a glass-topped table in the corner of a room.

Midwinter Magic in Summer

You know the strings of miniature lights that are hung on Christmas trees—a hundred magical little burning lights per string? Double and triple the strings and you have a wonderland of light.

If you have a balcony, get the kind of light strings that can go outdoors as well as inside. That way, if you're in the midsummer mood, you can visually expand the sense of space of a room with a balcony view by stringing lights you can see through your window. You can also hang miniature lights on outdoor plants and shrubbery or on a nearby tree.

THE LAZIEST WAY TO LIGHT YOUR HOME

Up to this point, I've shown you a lot of light sources and ways you can pool them into a lighting plan. Now you're probably thinking, "Cut to the chase: What's the fastest way I can get the job done, do it well, and not have it cost me major money?"

Take a quick inventory of the lighting in your home:

1. Inventory the general lighting in every room. That includes the daylight that comes in through the windows. Is there a room or two that depends on a plug-in light source for overall illumination?

2. List the tasks that take place in each room. Are there task lights that provide comfort for reading, cooking, office work, and looking in the mirror?

3. Do you have an area or two in the living or dining room that could use an accent light to show off a special collection or highlight a focal-point wall?

A list is half the plan. All that's left is to breeze through the following paragraphs and go shopping.

Count on Daylight

When you're short-circuiting traditional routes to a good lighting plan, sunlight is your greatest asset. Leave your windows as open and uncovered as possible to bring

YOU'LL THANK YOURSELF LATER

When you're buying bulbs or accent fixtures, remember that accent lighting requires three times the intensity of a room's general light to be effective.

daylight into your rooms. It will conserve electrical expenses and keep you walking around in natural light. Besides the obvious benefits of natural light, you'll have a more realistic view of your rooms and everyone in them. The yellowed light of incandescent bulbs or the bluish tones of fluorescence always puts a less-than-true color on things. Natural light is an especially good idea in dressing rooms and bathrooms, where you'd like to know the truth about how you look before you leave your home for the day.

Settle the General Score

If you have electricity in your home at all, you probably have plenty of general lighting. You also have sockets for quickly plugging in a portable floor lamp in a room without built-in overhead lights.

Your first priority is to fill in any missing general lighting needs. Using plug-in lighting is the fastest way to get the job done, and you'll find plenty of good floor lamps to buy. You could also consider killing two birds with one stone: A large table lamp with three-way switches and more than one bulb will give you general lighting and a good reading light, all in one fixture. You're already into the next step…task lighting!

It's a Portable Plan, Man

Quick-and-easy goes portable, so you don't need to wait for an electrician. All you need is a visit to a department, discount, or lighting store that supplies you with a variety of plug-in light sources in a style that fits your decor. Home

QUICK PAINLESS

Opaque shades bounce light off their surfaces, and translucent shades absorb and diffuse light in several directions. Use opaque shades for room darkening purposes and translucent ones for softening outdoor light.

centers probably won't have what you need. Their main fare is overhead lighting that's hung by an electrician.

Check your list to see how many lamps or types of lamps you're looking for. I've made my best lighting hits at large supermarket discount stores where housewares are a large part of the inventory. Prices are decent, and you can take all the time you like examining the packages and instructions to see how it all works. You'll also find suggestions for ways to use them on the lamp cartons.

Keep your priorities in this order:

1. General

2. Task

3. Accent

If you have to give up something for now, let it be the accent light. Accent lighting is mostly an aesthetic, a luxury light you can afford to wait on until it can be exactly as wonderful as you want it to be.

Choosing each lamp's style will be another issue. You might not find exactly the right thing in one-stop shopping. Again, hold off buying something that you don't really like. It'll just end up on the curb someday for the garbage man to pick up.

You can hope to get your lighting plan down in one fell swoop, but it's not terribly realistic. Look at it this way: It's all in the plan. The right lamp is out there waiting for you to discover it. You just need to keep your decorating eyes open while you're doing all your other more important things. Before you know it, the right lamp will

YOU'LL THANK YOURSELF LATER

When you're buying a new shade for your lamp, take the lamp base to the store to try some on. You'll save size and style mistakes and a lot of time.

Buy an adjustable pendant lamp to hang over your table. You can raise it for overall lighting or lower it for cozier gatherings. Look for a fixture that softens and diffuses the light so diners aren't blinded.

find you and you'll know it in an instant. Then, it's just a matter of taking it to its new home.

THE LOWDOWN ON LIGHT BULBS

The brightness and quality of light in your lamp or light fixture will vary with the bulb you choose. There are four choices:

- Incandescent: The most common of bulbs, this inexpensive, general-service light bulb produces a warm, yellowish-white light suitable for use in floor and table lamps and pendant fixtures. Although they are less expensive than halogen bulbs, they don't last as long.

- Reflectorized: These bulbs are incandescent bulbs with reflective coating inside. They give you about twice as much light as the general-service type bulb. They're good for spotlights and floodlights in situations where you need beam control.

- Fluorescent: Another common bulb, the fluorescent bulb casts a cool, bluish-white light. It's expensive, but it lasts about 20 times longer than the incandescent type. Use a compact fluorescent in conventional indoor fixtures.

- Halogen: These are expensive bulbs that produce a bright, white light that imitates natural daylight more closely than all other bulbs. They last a long time and produce more light per watt than incandescent bulbs, but don't place halogen lamps near curtains or other flammable materials.

Getting Time on Your Side

	The Old Way	The Lazy Way
Buying a lamp	3 trips to the store because you don't have a lighting plan	1 trip
Deciding what you need for lighting	Hours	A quick read of *The Lazy Way*
Buying the right shade for a lamp	2 or 3 trips	Take the lamp base with you; 1 trip
Creating a lighting plan	Days waiting for an electrician	Assemble it yourself with portable lighting
Getting the right lamp	Order it from a catalog; 2 months	Practice, patience, and let it cross your path
Creating special effects with lighting	30 minutes	3 minutes

*Frame a prized piece of furniture with a partial
accent wall in a hot-shot color. See Chapter 6.*
(King Au and Rebecca Jerdee)

*Sheers, slipcovers, and green plants keep your
rooms naturally light and relaxed.*
(King Au and Rebecca Jerdee)

*Air out a room by replacing pictures with mirrors
and filling a fireplace surround with another mirror.
See Chapter 12.*

(King Au and Rebecca Jerdee)

*In an intimate area, arrange pictures at eye level—
that's when you're seated.*

(King Au and Rebecca Jerdee)

Charm a guest room with repainted antique bed and a wispy canopy.
(King Au and Rebecca Jerdee)

Rest easy in a bed with duvet and a room with paper-thin shades.
(King Au and Rebecca Jerdee)

*Sleep in a white room with graceful tab-top curtains,
restful finishes, and bedside comforts.*
(King Au and Rebecca Jerdee)

*Toss a napkin on a tension rod for a curtain and
celebrate your instant genius. See Chapter 8.*
(King Au and Rebecca Jerdee)

Open shelves give you easy reaches and ready-made decorative objects.
(King Au and Rebecca Jerdee)

Rack your precious stemware and peg your jewelry. It adds up to storage with style. See Chapter 13.
(King Au and Rebecca Jerdee)

A convenient, serve-yourself cupboard keeps you from waiting on everyone.
(King Au and Rebecca Jerdee)

Slip a tiny storage cabinet and mirror in a hallway's almost-nothing space. See Chapter 13.
(King Au and Rebecca Jerdee)

Create a rose bowl in a compote for an intimate occasion. See Chapter 14.

(King Au and Rebecca Jerdee)

Bathroom storage doubles as decoration.

(King Au and Rebecca Jerdee)

Mirrors double the number of flower blossoms you place in front of them. See Chapter 14.
(King Au and Rebecca Jerdee)

Hooks and shelves with small containers that organize the little stuff keep you free from desperate searches. See Chapter 13.
(King Au and Rebecca Jerdee)

Chapter

ten

Fast Furniture Fix-Ups

In the language of lazy, hard-work words such as "refinish" and "reupholster" are pronounced "renew," "refresh," and "relax." Lazy leaves heavy-duty furniture fix-ups to heavy-duty furniture folks whose full-time occupations keep them into serious upholstery and wood refinishing. In the relaxed realm of *The Lazy Way*, you want fast furniture fix-ups that don't cost you a lot in money or time.

This chapter is not about the daunting prospect of buying and arranging furniture. (You can get all that information from *The Complete Idiot's Guide to Decorating Your Home* by Alpha Books.) I'm here to talk about the furniture you already have, whether you're starting your first home or readying your last one for retirement. I show you stress-free ways to redecorate upholstered furniture, put a fast finish on wood or iron, and turn complicated bed making into a one-minute deal.

HOME ON THE STAGE

I like to think of creating a home and each room in it as putting together a theatre set for staging a play. Each room has three layers:

■ Backgrounds: Walls (with doors, windows, and curtains), a floor, and a textured ceiling (including lights) are the backdrops for staging each room. Sometimes, the backdrops are dramatic; sometimes, they're barely there.

■ Furniture: In each room, the building blocks of living are arranged in a sort of stage setting so that life can be comfortably played out. You create your sets for living with the building blocks of sofas, chairs, storage pieces, tables, and beds. Furniture, the most serviceable elements of a room, must fit and comfort the bodies in your house. Choose them for comfort first and then style. Arrange them so they're easily accessible and looking good enough for company—an audience for your decorating act.

■ Accessories: The small things—lamps, books, trunks, trays, pillows, flowers, dishes, and candles—are the "props" for each room's stage. Useful as they are for eating, drinking, reading, sleeping, and bathing, they also carry your personal style and signature, simply by the way you choose and arrange them.

Except for storage pieces (also known as case goods by furniture manufacturers), your home has three types

of furniture that could probably use a little lazy redecorating:

- Sofas and chairs
- Tables
- Beds

Whether you're looking for quick answers on prevention or removal or easy cover-ups for persistent upholstery stains, you'll probably find something useful in this chapter. You'll also find ideas for fixing niggling little wood finish problems, a way to assemble a small table from scratch, and the ultimate in lazy bed making. But first, the laziest trick of all.

A Fluid Ounce of Stain Prevention

Protect your upholstery fabrics before stains happen. It'll buy you some time before you have to do something serious about fixing up your furniture.

You'll need

Chair or sofa upholstered in new or newly cleaned, natural or synthetic colorfast fabric (not leather, vinyl, suede, imitation suede, or carpet)

Fabric protector in an aerosol dispenser

1 Read and follow the instructions and precautions on the container.

2 Turn the spray button to the "on" position.

3 Spray with a sweeping motion six inches from the fabric with a speed that will evenly wet the fabric. Overlap the spray areas.

4 Allow the fabric to dry for up to six hours before using the furniture.

5 Test for repellency with a few drops of water. If water soaks in, add more protector.

When liquids or spills fall onto the fabric, they'll blot up before they turn into stains. A quick wipe with an absorbent cloth, and the would-be stains are gone.

STAGE COMPLAINTS

You can hear the chairs and sofa whining in the background like little debutantes at the ball that want to be the center of every conversation and the murmur in every lover's heart. Like the aging dance master who's showing the cracks and wearing down after a thousand performances.

The Rain in Spain

Your brand-new armchair is begging for a new look. Already. It's not the chair's fault; it's yours. You're the one who left the window open while you ran out for an evening. It's still sitting there where you left it to dry after a thunderstorm drenched it. Now, it's sporting a great big rain stain half the size of Australia. It's been weeks now, and the sobbing sounds are getting louder every day. You can't afford a new upholstery job just yet. Besides, you can't live without the chair at this point in your life.

A temporary solution might tide you over: Wrap your chair in a decorative chair throw. It works in much the same way as a flat sheet you fold and wrap around your mattress.

Old Faithful

It's had a long life of service so it's not surprising that your sofa's looking a trifle dingy and feeling in need of attention. You argue that it's not so dingy that it needs expensive upholstery. You've tried spot removers and patiently wiped up spills as soon as they happen, but the nagging little shadows of former stains are getting on your nerves.

Solution: Slip readymade slipcovers over your sofa to fit in much the same way as fitted sheets do on your bed. A little elastic here, a little there, and you've given old faithful a new lease on life.

YOU'LL THANK YOURSELF LATER

Get estimates on what it would cost to reupholster a chair or sofa professionally. You'll save time deciding whether you should do something about it.

Hot Seats

Your dining room chairs have been sat out and ground down to a miserable remnant of what they used to be. Your dinner party's coming up and your back's against the wall.

Possible solution: Check under the seat pads to see if they're attached to the chair by screws. If they are, you've got removable seats and you can do something about it yourself. Borrow or rent a power stapler and get someone to help you re-wrap the seats in new fabric.

There's nothing new about slipcovers or chair throws. My mother had them in the 40s—big, flowery cabbage-rose prints that matched her cabbage-rose draperies. In the 90s, slipcovers were trendy, going as loose and relaxed as they possibly could and appearing in every mail-order catalog and home store in the country. Even Target, Kmart, and Wal-Mart expanded their housewares departments to include new wrinkly cotton and chenille covers.

I purchased fitted cotton canvas covers for my loveseats when I bought them and I've never been sorry. Sometimes, my sofas go bare for a season, and when I tire of the tight, upholstered look, I loosen it with freshly laundered slipcovers I don't have to iron. (We're accustomed to the wrinkled look by now.)

LOOSE SLIPS

The commitment level here is low. You can buy loose throws for as little as $30 or a quality throw that costs a lot more. Whether you're tossing on an inexpensive wrap or going the expensive route, the process is the same.

IF YOU'RE SO INCLINED

Toss on a throw, slide a decorative runner over the back of chair, fit on a slip, and re-wrap a dining-chair seat.

Chair Throw

Furniture throws come in several sizes, depending on where you shop. A chair throw for covering a 32 × 40-inch chair measures 70 × 90 inches. A loveseat throw is 70 × 140 inches, and a sofa throw grows to a 70 × 170-inch size. Most are machine-washable in cotton or polyester/cotton blends.

To fit a throw to a chair, you'll need

Chair
Chair throw
Package illustration
Your hands

1 Center the throw on the chair so all sides are even to the floor. If your chair is higher than 32 inches, set the throw forward so that it covers the front of the chair fully. (You can hide the back of the chair from view.)

2 Smooth the throw over the seat and tuck the fabric down around the cushion.

3 Push and tuck the fabric into the corners where the back and arms meet.

Easy Runner

This project is for a fully upholstered dining room chair or a chair with an upholstered seat and back that you'd like to disguise. The clever device: A long, readymade table runner that works like a sleeveless tunic, or tabard. It's an especially nice look if each end of the runner comes to a point and is finished with a tassel.

You'll need

Chair

13 × 72-inch table runner

1 Lay the runner tentatively over the chair from front to back.

2 Adjust the length until it hangs gracefully down the back and the front of the chair.

3 With your fingers, push the runner into the crevice where the seat and back meet.

4 Push the fabric as deeply into the crevice as possible to ensure that it won't slip out when someone sits on it.

TIGHT FITS

If you're looking for a more secure slipcover fit or tight upholstery, you have about five options:

- Do a semi-fit job yourself with readymade slipcovers you buy in a home store.

- Buy a readymade, tight-fitting slipcover made especially for your specific piece of new furniture. Purchase it from the manufacturer of your furniture.

- Custom-order a slipcover for an old sofa through an interior design service.

- Do simple seat-cover upholstery yourself.

- Commit a piece of furniture to an upholsterer after you've chosen fabric and received an estimate of the costs.

The price for a semi-fit will be right on the package, and you'll know what you're getting into when you hold the package in your hand. No hassle.

Custom-order isn't as hassle-free. You'll need to get someone to give you an estimate before you commit, or you could get yourself into an expense you can't really afford. However, if you can afford it, the custom-order will give you long-term satisfaction if you can get exactly what you want.

Slip It a Semi-Fit

The instructions here are for semi-fitted readymade slipcovers that will fit your furniture approximately. Buy machine-washable covers with elasticized edges that will hold without pins (a safety hazard). Some slipcover styles have handsome flat ties that secure the cover at each corner of the sofa or chair.

You'll need

Semi-fitted slipcover set

Package instructions (often in picture form)

1. Start at one side of the chair or sofa, fitting it over the arm, front, and back.

2. Move to the center, and pull the cover across the back and seat.

3. If the slipcover has elastic to hold it in place, position the elastic gathers along the edge of the seat at the bottom or under the arms at the sides.

4. Pull the slipcover completely over the chair on the opposite side.

YOU'LL THANK YOURSELF LATER

Before you shop for a slipcover, measure your furniture piece so you know how high, wide, and deep it is.

Taut Seats: Reviving a Dining Chair

You're committed to the time it takes to upholster a dining-chair seat? It'll take you about an hour for each one if you have someone to help. Doing it alone is difficult, but possible.

You'll need

Screwdriver

Pliers

Power staple gun (rent from tool-rental store or borrow from a woodworking friend)

Staples to fit the staple gun

Upholstery fabric with sturdy backing (purchase at a fabric store)

Fabric shears

Straight pins (for sewing)

Someone to help you

1 Unscrew the seats from the dining room chairs with the screwdriver.

2 Lift the staples from the chair seat bottom with a screwdriver.

3 Pull away the old covering with pliers.

4 Use the old seat top as a pattern for the new seat cover.

5 Pin the old seat onto the new fabric with the pins. (Be sure the grain of the fabric runs from the back of the chair to the front.)

A COMPLETE WASTE OF TIME

The 3 Worst Things to Do When Re-covering a Dining Chair Seat:

1. Cover over old, worn-down padding.

2. Choose stretchy fabric without a backing.

3. Staple around the chair seat instead of working the upholstery from back to front and from side to side.

6 Cut out the seat cover.

7 Position the new cover on the chair seat.

8 Turn it over and staple the raw edges of the fabric onto the chair bottom in the following sequence: a) Put the first staple at the center of the seat back. b) Pull the fabric taut over the front of the seat and put in the second staple. c) Repeat the process on one side. d) Repeat on the other side.

9 Continue pulling the raw edges taut around the seat while someone else staples them down. In each section between staples, work from the center of the section toward one staple and then toward the other. Repeat for each section.

10 Reattach the seat to the chair with the screwdriver.

FAST FINISHES

Rub-on oils and spray-on paints are the fastest way to furniture finishes. All the products come with instructions on the packaging so you'll know what you're committing to before you ever turn over the cash.

Tung Oil

This easy-to-apply tung oil finish is a drying oil obtained from the seeds of a Chinese tree that now grows in the southern United States. Tung oil creates a remarkably durable, hand-rubbed luster but takes only minutes to apply. It's the ideal protective finish for woods that have been refinished because

Bravo! If you've re-covered your dining room seats, you've just pulled off the most difficult project in this book. It's dinner out for you and your sidekick.

The Lazy Way

QUICK ⚫ PAINLESS

it penetrates wood pores and restores vitality to dry, thirsty wood. You can use it over stained wood or apply it on raw wood. Don't apply it on surfaces already sealed with a protective finish; it won't penetrate.

To shine up a new, unstained piece of furniture or one that's not sealed with a varnish, you'll need

Furniture piece

Sandpaper

Tack cloth

Tung oil

Cheesecloth

Foam brush (optional)

Clean, lint-free cloth

1 Sand the furniture surfaces smooth.

2 Wipe away sanding dust with the tack cloth.

3 Wipe on a generous coat of oil in the direction of the grain with a cheesecloth—or brush it on with the foam brush.

4 After 5 or 10 minutes, buff the surfaces evenly with a clean, lint-free cloth. If buffing is difficult, re-coat the surface immediately and buff.

5 For additional body and gloss, repeat Steps 3 and 4 after 24 hours.

Refresh your wood surfaces periodically with tung oil to keep them looking glossy.

Quick-Chrome

Take metallic-chrome–colored spray paint to the beaten-down surfaces of well-used furniture, and it'll be ready for the brand-new millennium. I'm particularly fond of the results I got from this fast-and-easy process on a broken-down, hand-me-down iron bed frame I was given. Try it. You'll like it. The sleek look of shiny chrome is especially surprising and fun on country-style ladder-back chairs with rush or wicker seats. The rough, earthy fibers on the seats contrast dramatically with the outer-space look of sleek chrome.

Choose a secondhand furniture piece that's seen better days. You can chrome wood or metal with good results if you clean the surfaces before you begin.

To give a furniture piece a new coat of chrome, you'll need

Wood or metal furniture piece

Sand paper

Soap and water

Rags

An outdoor work space

Newspapers

Spray primer

Fast-drying, rust-inhibiting interior/exterior metallic chrome spray paint

1 Remove all grease, oil, dirt, wax, and rust scale from the surface before you take it outdoors.

2 Sand it smooth.

IF YOU'RE SO
INCLINED

You love the high speed of spray painting and can't stop? It's your call. Paint accessories (lamp bases, a side table, or a wicker chair) that live in the same room to match the big furniture piece you just completed.

3 Wash away small dust particles with soap and water.

4 Air-dry for an hour.

5 Working outdoors if possible, spread newspapers over your work area to keep the spray residue from filtering onto the ground.

6 Prime new and bare metal surfaces.

7 Shake the metallic paint can for two minutes before painting and occasionally during use. Hold the spray can 10 to 12 inches from the surface and apply a thin coat.

8 Re-coat within an hour.

THE LAZY BED

The lazy bed is only easy to make; it's not easy to get out of.

It has four bed-making parts:

- A fitted bottom sheet: A large rectangular piece of linen, cotton, or a blend of other material used for making a bed. Its corners are stitched to wrap tightly around the mattress.

- A duvet: A comforter filled with down or a polyester blend. Stitching holds the filling in place. For a down-filled duvet, you can choose from a tight or loose cover construction. Baffle covers contain the fill in tightly walled squares, keeping the loft (or thickness) high and balanced. Channel construction or ring stitching allows you to shift the duvet contents and vary the concentration of warmth. Although not as warm or natural, non-allergenic down alternatives are available. Synthetic, wool, and cotton downs weigh more but have the advantage of being washable. Silk-filled comforters are warmer, more lightweight, and more expensive.

- A duvet cover: A large, rectangular fabric envelope (like a pillowcase) that slips over the duvet to keep it clean. You can close the end where you slip in the duvet with ties, Velcro, or snaps. You can buy a duvet in silk, polyester blends, cotton sheet-like fabrics, or cozy, comfortable knitted T-shirt fabric.

- Pillows and pillow covers.

Leaving Out the Layers

The lazy bed is a simple one because it eliminates many layers of blankets, a bedspread, and a top sheet. If you're tired of making your bed the complicated way, try The Lazy Way.

You'll need

Fitted sheet to fit your bed
Duvet that's at least 18 inches wider than your bed
Duvet cover to fit the duvet
Pillows (optional)
Pillowcases (optional)
Someone to help

1. Pull the fitted sheet over your mattress. (A mattress pad over the mattress is a good idea.)

YOU'LL THANK YOURSELF LATER

To protect your lazy intentions, keep the KISS word (Keep it Simple, Stupid) in your heart at all times.

2 Open the duvet cover and arrange it on the bed with its open end (the bottom) between you and your friend at the head of the bed.

3 Lay the duvet over the cover with the duvet bottom lying over the open end of the cover.

4 Take one top corner of the duvet in your right hand and the corresponding corner of the duvet in your left.

5 Your friend is doing the same thing on the other side of the bed with the opposite top corners.

6 Hold the left corner of the duvet cover while you enter the opening of the cover with the duvet corner held in your right hand.

7 Put the two corners together (your friend is doing the same thing at the same time on the other side), grasp them both in your left hand, and, with your right hand, pull the duvet cover down around the duvet—back toward the head of the bed.

8 Match the bottom corners as you did for the top of the duvet.

9 Close the duvet.

10 Holding a top corner in your left hand and a bottom corner in your right (your friend's doing the same) shake the duvet inside the cover to balance the loft.

11 Flop it over and fluff it onto the bed over the fitted sheet.

12 Add the pillows, if you use them.

Making the lazy bed

1 Get out of bed.

2 Fluff the duvet in the air and let it fall on the bed.

3 Toss the pillow at the top of the bed.

Lazy Side Table

For a simple answer to a need for a bedside or chair-side table, try the round, fabric-covered decorator table. It's available everywhere in a 20- or 24-inch diameter round top and measures 24 inches high. You can find it in fabric stores, import stores, and discount stores, and it'll cost you little more than $15 or $20 to assemble. If you want, you can buy a $6 to $10 glass top for it. Add the cost of covering it with fabric, and you're still under $50. Assembly time will be about three minutes.

Shop the housewares section of a discount store, and you'll see everything you need in one place:

Decorator table set (tabletop round, three attachable dowel-rod legs)

Round table covering to fit (they'll be hanging near the wood table sets)

Glass top (optional)

IF YOU'RE SO INCLINED

Rub a little tung oil on your decorator table's legs if it's showing a little leg. (That's if you covered the table with a short 36- or 42-inch square cloth.)

1 Open the carton and examine the pieces.

2 Screw the legs into the notches on the bottom of the table-top.

3 Cover the table with the tablecloth. (Steam out the wrinkles in the shower, if necessary.)

4 Add the glass top.

5 Clean the glass top with glass cleaner and paper towels before you arrange a lamp and other accessories on the table.

Once furniture pieces set your stage, you can fine-tune your rooms with accessories that make it personally yours. The next chapter, picture arranging, and the rest of the book show you fine-tuning The Lazy Way.

Getting Time on Your Side

	The Old Way	**The Lazy Way**
Removing a stain	Scrub-a-dub-dub	A few-second wipe-up
Making a bed	10 minutes	1 minute
Staining a piece of furniture	1 hour	20 minutes
Reupholstering a sofa	A few weeks at the upholsterer's	An hour plus a trip to the store
Building a table	Make it from scratch in about 2 weeks	5 minutes
Finding a solution for stains	Days scratching your head	A quick read of this book

Painless Picture Arranging

Pictures have a way of dropping into your hands and inviting themselves right into your house. It's like falling in love; when your eyes see what your heart desires, it follows that the objects of your attention will eventually become yours. In a single lifetime, thousands of images will touch places in your heart and find their way home.

Pictures window your world, or, at least, the world as you know it. Inevitably, you collect pictures that recapture places you've visited (or haven't), people you've known, and times you'd like to remember. Sometimes, you choose a picture for no reason except that it struck your fancy or jump-started your heart.

Hanging it all is a *commitment*—fightin' words for *The Lazy Way* fan. Okay, we'll go easy. We'll go tentative and temporary, at least for a little while—until you're more comfortable with the idea of pounding nails in your walls and committing to re-organizing your pictures.

TENTATIVELY SPEAKING

Your picture collection probably consists of snapshots and posters, picture books, postcards, home-store prints, and art shop originals. Add to that collection—watercolors you've swapped with a friend, a long trail of kids' school drawings, family pictures framed in precious frames—and you have enough pictorial material to open a gallery. Your picture displays probably fall into categories such as these:

- Kitchen gallery: When you don't know what to do with favorite snapshots, another child's drawing, or a Boy Scouts crafts project, you arrange them all in a giant magnetic collage on the refrigerator door.

- Scrapbooks and files: Some filled, some waiting to be filled. It's okay. There's always time.

- Family gallery: You've framed a few images that represent the bigger moments of your life in small decorative frames and arranged them on an end table.

- Poster images: Sometimes, you or others in your house tack posters on a bulletin board, a wall, or even a ceiling.

- Large framed prints and paintings: Find hooks for them on the wall over the sofa and the bed.

- The archives: Here lies the bulk of your intentions— the closet of pictures needing frames and places, pictures used and put away, and pictures someone gave you that you're not ready to hang. Under the bed is another good place to stack picture upon picture upon picture.

It's not a bad start. Now, it's just a short distance to fine-tuning your picture-arranging habits.

TEMPORARY MEASURES

Common sense is a good picture-arranging guide. If you feel like putting off permanent placements, have some easy arranging fun in the meantime. These quick-and-easy arranging tactics let you enjoy your pictures while you study them, decide which ones deserve framing (if any), and determine which ones will remain in the archives forever.

- Picture ledges: Window seats, mantels, shelves, and chair-rail ledges give you places to set your pictures upright so you can stand back, view them at a distance, notice which picture looks good with another.

- Tabletop displays: Desktops, bureau tops, round tables, and end tables give you places to stand your unabashedly sentimental collection of tenderly framed family photos.

- Floor displays: A floor where you can stand back for a good, long view is a good starting point for sizing up your big pictures.

When you're ready to move on, the projects on the following pages will help you fine-tune your tentative arrangements and help you cut back on the overflow.

Sort your pictures to get an inventory of your picture-arranging potential. Keep snapshots and small pictures in a small container, prints and posters between large sheets of cardboard, and framed pieces together in one spot.

Snapshot Gallery

If you're one of those picture arrangers who plasters snapshots and everything else on your refrigerator doors, practice your picture-arranging skills right there. Here's a series of snapshot showings to schedule on your refrigerator door. Each showing reflects a miniature picture-arranging principle that you can use later when arranging larger pictures in your rooms.

Imagine the freezer door (the upper portion of your refrigerator) as a wall for display. If you have a side-by-side refrigerator, use one door or the other, and arrange your pictures vertically instead of horizontally. Remove the clutter to get a fresh, new gallery wall, and arrange snapshots in the following sequences.

You'll need

Regular and jumbo snapshots

Adhesive-backed magnetic tape (available at crafts supply stores)

Scissors

To prepare the snapshots for hanging, follow these steps:

1 Cut the magnetic tape into small squares.

2 Remove the paper backing from the magnetic squares and adhere a square to each corner of a snapshot. (Put one in the middle for additional support, if desired.)

Use these instructions for preparing your snapshots. Then, follow these instructions to arrange them.

Single Snap

Choose one outstanding piece and arrange it formally or casually. For a formal look, place it dead center on the door like a target. For a casual look, place it either to the right or the left side of the door so that the margins on each side of the picture are unequal but pleasantly balanced.

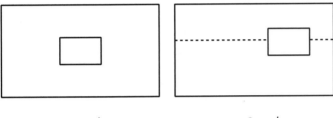

Formal   Casual

Twin Snaps

Choose two pictures of similar content that complement each other and arrange them formally or casually. Equal sizes suggest a formal arrangement, so place them side-by-side in the center of the door. Then, shift them upward a few inches so that the top and bottom margins above and below the pictures are unequal but pleasantly balanced.

Snapshots of two different sizes create a casual pair. To arrange them, follow these suggestions:

- Place the larger one to the lower right of the freezer door, keeping the white margins around the picture arrangement pleasantly balanced.

QUICK ⬢ PAINLESS

Shoot a couple of rolls of film for your snapshot gallery and get one roll printed in jumbo sizes, the other regular. This will give you a fresh selection without having to stir through your snapshot archives.

■ Place the smaller photo with its top edge an inch or so higher than the top edge of the larger one. The space between the photos should be the same measurement as the inch or so that the small photo rises above the larger one.

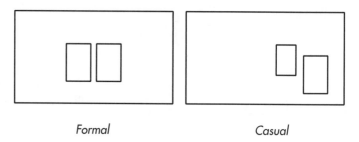

Formal   Casual

Three's Company

Choose three snapshots that tell a story when combined. Give them a formal gallery line-up: To place them, draw an imaginary horizontal line across the freezer door an inch or two above the center. (If you have a vertical door, draw a vertical line.) Whether the pictures are tall or wide, center them on the imagined line.

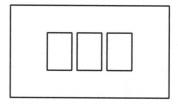

Three's company

Four on a Grid

Arrange four snapshots in a formal grid for big impact. To do so, start with four pictures of the same size and cluster them together in a tightly knit group. Keep all the spaces between the pictures the same and narrow enough (about a half inch or so) so that the pictures work together as a strong group rather than as four separate pictures competing for attention.

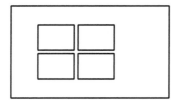

Four on a grid

Five's an Odd Number

Choose five pictures (odd numbers are often more playful and casual than even-numbered arrangements) of different sizes. One picture should be larger than the others and the sizes of the other pictures not radically different from the large one:

- Place the largest picture (the focal point because of its size) to the right or to the left of the freezer door, just above center.

- Arrange the remaining snapshots to either side, above, or below it, balancing the sizes of the spaces between the pictures with the sizes of the pictures.

IF YOU'RE SO
INCLINED

Add a decorative flourish to your refrigerator arrangement of five pieces—an eye-catching magnet on a corner of the starring-role snapshot—to give it extra status.

At this point, the process is guided only by intuition—what looks and feels right. The purpose of this arrangement is to keep the focal point picture in the primary position whereas all other pictures play supporting roles.

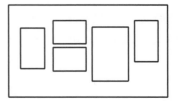

Five's an odd number

Then, There Were Six

With six equal-sized horizontal pictures or six equal-sized vertical pictures, arrange two tiers of three pictures each. Keep the spaces between them equal and fairly close. Keep the margins around the entire group equal.

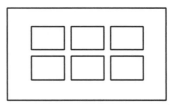

Then, there were six

Seven's heaven. Take a rest. Keep these picture-arranging principles in mind when you hang large pictures in permanent arrangements.

YOU'LL THANK YOURSELF LATER

Save money by purchasing an inexpensive readymade frame for a print, but spend money on a large, custom-order mat to give it more size.

Pushpin Gallery

You know the kids' drawings that keep coming home from school? Don't put them on the refrigerator door anymore. Give them a better life at the pushpin gallery. Your kids will attach more worth to their art works if you give them special showings. Just keep it moving: When a new piece is added, an old one goes to the archives.

You'll need

Self-adhesive cork tile (available at lumberyard stores in the tile sections)

Pushpins

1 Hang a border of cork tile 30 inches from the floor on a wall in a hall or room where everyone will notice the pictures. (Instructions will come with your tile.)

2 Hang the pictures on the cork border with metal or plastic pushpins. (If you have babies in the house, take safety measures.)

Tabletop Story

There's not a lot of cutting back to do when it comes to framed family pictures and important moments. Sheer emotional attachments override the less-is-more philosophy, and that's well within the laws of picture arranging. Sometimes, more is more.

Only one thing could give your family pictures more dignity and worth as a group: Frames of one type of material. Don't mix wood and plastic or brass with glass. Decide on one kind of material for your family frames and stick with it.

Give your kids the assignment of hanging the refrigerator snap-shot gallery showings while you sit back and watch. You'll both learn something, and you won't have to do anything.

The Lazy Way

You can choose from

Wood	Brass
Plastic	Pewter
Shell	Galvanized metal
Silver	Wrought iron
Gold	

1 Choose one picture to anchor your tabletop arrangement. Usually, a large size or exaggerated frame will make a picture the star of a group.

2 Set the "star" near the largest object on the table. (A lamp is a good starting point.)

3 Arrange the second largest pictures around it in supporting positions—not too close, not too far. Use your intuition for balancing picture sizes and spaces.

4 Tuck the tiny pieces into the leftover spaces, linking them with the secondary pictures by overlapping their corners.

Ledge Sitters

You can create simple galleries and change them on a whim. Deep window seats or wall-hung picture ledges you order from catalogs work well. Other places to find ledges are in a bookcase or on a mantel.

To avoid a cluttered look, choose pictures of similar content framed in the same type of frame. For example, choose all black and white photographs framed in black metal contemporary frames for a graphic look. For a softer look, choose sepia-toned portraits framed in simple birch frames.

You'll need

Pictures framed in the same material

Ledges

A curved vase of flowers (to counteract all the hard edges
of the frames)

1 Line up your pictures on the ledge. Which one wants to be
the focus of the arrangement?

2 Place the focal-point frame to the right or to the left of the
center of the ledge.

3 Arrange subordinate pictures on either side, overlapping
some.

4 Open a space near the focal-point piece.

5 Place the curved flower arrangement in the space so that
it links both sides of the picture line-up.

With bookcase ledges, avoid scattering frames in between
books (it makes a cluttered look). Instead, choose one level of
bookshelves for your pictures and move out the books to make
room for them.

Floor Show

*You can make a big-picture review on the floor by leaning
your posters, prints, and paintings against the wall. Choose a
floor where the view is long and far away so you'll have a
good chance to see the whole line-up.*

IF YOU'RE SO
INCLINED

Once you decide what
material you'd like for
your frames, tell every-
one you know about it.
That way, if someone
wants to give you a gift
of a framed family photo,
it'll fit in.

You'll need

Your art collection

An easel

1 Line up the pictures on the floor, overlapping and arranging them tentatively.

2 Pare down the pieces that don't fit with the group because they stand out and aren't joined by a common theme.

3 Find a common theme for your gallery arrangement.

4 Place the easel at a focal point spot somewhere along the wall where it won't be tripped over.

5 Place the focal-point print or painting on the easel, giving it height and power but relating it to the rest. (You might have to lower the ledge on the easel.)

6 Whittle down the arrangement to only those pictures that don't weaken the entire group.

SEMI-PERMANENT MEASURES

No picture hanging is ever permanent. Sooner or later, your tastes will change and a new style of pictures will pull at your heartstrings or trip your trigger.

The two picture-hanging projects that follow on the next few pages suggest dry mounting your print images instead of fitting them with glass. Dry mounting keeps large pictures sturdy yet casual and lightweight, fairly inexpensive, and easily transportable, and you don't have to worry about broken glass.

QUICK ☜☞ PAINLESS

To more easily coordinate your collection, choose pictures that have something in common—color, image, or theme.

Dry mounting is a framing process that fastens a sturdy foam core board to the back of a print or poster to make it firm enough to stand on its own. This makes it possible to frame the firmed-up picture without a piece of glass in front of it to keep it flat in the frame. You can order dry mounting at most frame shops. It costs about half the amount of framing a picture with glass.

Poster Child

Personally, I've never moved beyond the poster age. I think you're supposed to do that just about the time you get out of college and move into your first real apartment or home. At that point, you upgrade your art collection.

I love the finer stuff but don't have the tolerance for it in my house. For some reason, when I bring home a grown-up painting and hang it on the wall, it feels too important, too heavy and serious for my lightweight nature and spaces. It walks right in and takes over the room, and I'm hounded by its presence every time I go near it.

I've given myself permission to live with posters that suit my easy-going attitude. I can change them from time to time when my decorating moods shift. I leave serious art pieces to museums and galleries where I can visit them. At home, I live with Holly-Go-Lightly pictures that reflect my taste. At the moment, Matisse is my painterly love. I find his posters lively and free of heavy messages and statements I have to digest.

IF YOU'RE SO
INCLINED

Visit a museum shop after seeing a gallery exhibit. You'll find large files of posters and prints you can take home.

Doing the Most with a Poster

If you're still in the poster and print stage, don't apologize. Here's how to treat a poster like a piece of art and give it the status it deserves.

You'll need

Dry-mounted poster (available at framing shops)

Frame kit to fit the poster (available at art and framing supply stores)

Picture-hanging kit (wire, nail, hook)

Wire cutters

Someone to help you

Pencil

Ruler

Hammer

1 Assemble the frame around the poster by following the instructions that come with the kit.

2 Cut a length of picture wire eight inches longer than the width of the span across the back of the poster.

3 Slip the wire ends through the hanging hooks on the frame and twist them back onto the wire to secure.

4 Ask someone to hold the poster for you while you decide exactly where you'll hang it.

5 Mark the wall lightly with a pencil along the top and center of the frame.

6 Hold the hanging wire taut and measure from the frame top to the center hanging point of the wire.

7 Mark the hanging point on the wall below the first mark using the measurement in Step 6.

8 Pound in the hanging hook.

9 Adjust the level of the poster by shifting the wire along the hanging hook.

Two's Company

When two pictures are better than one, the picture hanging gets a little trickier. If you follow the instructions here and measure carefully, you won't end up with a wall full of holes.

To hang a side-by-side pair, you'll need

Two dry-mounted prints or posters of the same size and similar content

Two frame kits to fit the posters

Picture-hanging kit (wire, two hooks, two nails)

Wire cutters

Someone to help you

Pencil

Ruler

Carpenter's level

Hammer

1 Frame the prints following the frame kit's instructions.

2 Add the hanging wires to the backs of the frames using the instructions supplied on the picture-hanging kit. Position them exactly alike on the backs of the frames to make picture hanging easier.

YOU'LL THANK YOURSELF LATER

When hanging a large picture over a sofa, hang it just high enough (4–6 inches) above the sofa so you don't hit your head when sitting but not so high that it seems uncomfortably detached.

QUICK ☞ PAINLESS

3 Ask your friend to hold the pair of prints while you decide exactly where you'll hang them. Then, have him or her put down one frame while you hang the other.

4 Mark the wall lightly with a pencil at the top center of the frame.

5 Measure from the frame top to the center of the hanging wire. (Hold the wire taut as if it were hung.)

6 Mark the wall below the first mark using the measurement in Step 5. This is where the picture hook goes.

7 Pound in the picture hook with the hammer.

8 Hang the frame on the hook.

9 Be sure the second frame's hanging wire is positioned on the back of the frame exactly as the first one.

10 Ask your friend to hold the second frame against the wall.

11 Use the level to determine whether the top of the second frame is level with the first.

12 Repeat Steps 6 and 7 to hang the second frame.

Have a totally stress-free Lazy Way picture-arranging experience: Don't consider your arrangements permanent. Try out your pictures, see how they look in different places, and live with them for a while; then, decide their decorative destinies.

Getting Time on Your Side

	The Old Way	The Lazy Way
Framing a picture	Weeks at the frame shop	20 minutes
Hanging a picture	Days thinking about it	10 minutes
Deciding which pictures to hang	Paralyzed by the fear of making a decision	It's okay to change your mind
Re-hanging a picture	Twice (You hung it too high)	No re-hanging (You hung it at eye level)
Practicing your arranging skills	On a wall you riddle with nail holes	On the refrigerator with magnets
Losing sleep over picture hanging	Nightmares	Sweet dreams

Mirror Magic

If it weren't for mirrors, we'd all turn into toads. We'd be oblivious to bad-hair days and bristly chins and go for years without knowing that a little makeup could work wonders. The fairest mirrors in our houses are the ones that are there when we need them, telling us the bold-faced truth without getting smart.

Besides their obvious function of letting us check our good looks in their smooth, quiet surfaces, the glittering presence of mirrors brings a lightness of being, a sense of refinement, and the illusion of larger living space to our rooms.

Ask a mirror what it sees, and it'll answer right back. Not only does it tell you how you look, its frame tells everyone else about your style and taste in decorating.

WHAT'S IN THE LOOKING GLASS

What you see is what you get. It's an uncomplicated affair, really—a piece of glass hung in a frame. Long ago and far away, mirrors were made from pieces of metal so highly polished that they reflected images (as long as it was outdoors on

a clear day). Now that reflective surfaces are created from slick, smooth glass, they give a true picture of what they see.

Parts Is Parts

If you've never examined a mirror closely, you've missed its simple construction and these easy-to-remember parts:

- A glass surface with a metallic or amalgam backing that causes the glass to reflect: It can be flat-planed or curved in a convex or concave surface.

- A frame that protects a mirror's glass edges from cutting into other objects and cracking: (Who needs a cracked mirror?). It also gives style to an ordinary piece of glass and supplies a surface for attaching a hanger. The glass is fastened into the frame with glazier's metal points or strong adhesive.

- A hanger on the reverse side—usually a wire, loop, saw-tooth bar, or clips fastened to the wall: Mirrors affixed to a wall permanently are glued on with a mastic made especially for mirror surfaces.

What Mirrors Do

Mirrors make your rooms come alive. A home without a mirror is like a wall without windows. Without either, the air seems dead and still.

Here's a list of wonderful things mirrors do for you:

- Keep you looking good: Lately, I've been avoiding bright, new mirrors and looking at myself only in ones with aged surfaces like mine. Old mirrors don't seem to notice my wrinkles, and it comforts me to share a moment with them.

- Enlarge living spaces: Okay, they don't actually *do* it; it's just an illusion, like what *Alice in Wonderland* sees through her looking glass. The reflection makes you feel as if you're seeing the whole room.

- Double the light (did I say double de-light?): Like everything else they reflect, mirrors beam back window light with twice the power and impact.

- Add sparkle and shine: Big or small, the smooth surface of a mirror contrasts with most other textures in a room.

- Add architecture: Large, oversized mirrors are like additional windows that bring a certain style to the rest of the decorating scheme. Their frames, like those on windows and doors, are the bones of a room.

SO MANY SIZES, SHAPES, AND STYLES—SO LITTLE SPACE

When you're redecorating, think less about the shape of a mirror and more about its size and the style of frame it carries. Mirrors can range from oversized major statements dredged up from salvage warehouses to some so tiny you can hold them in the palm of your hand.

Consider these choices when you're incorporating mirrors in your redecorating scheme:

- Oversize mirrors (sometimes known as *pier mirrors*) come in frames so large that they really work best

IF YOU'RE SO
INCLINED

Highlight an old window's architecture by replacing its glass with a new mirror.

Before you hang an arrangement of small mirrors on a wall, try it on the floor beneath the space. You'll eliminate a lot of practice nail holes.

standing on the floor propped up against a wall. In this angled position, they reflect the airier, upper parts of a room. Currently, they are the big-impact redecorating favorite.

- Full-length mirrors are standard fare for every home. You can choose a strictly practical version with a beveled edge to clip to a door or wall. You can also choose a simply framed one for the same reason. When added style is important to you, choose a full-length mirror that's set into a freestanding frame.

- Vanity mirrors, the most common type used in bathrooms and other private spaces, come in everything from mirror tile, which is glued to an entire wall, to a single antique square that hangs over a chest of drawers.

- Magnifying mirrors on extension arms attached to bathroom walls are coming back in reproduction styles that are truly appealing.

- Decorative mirrors are valued more for their own good looks than for practical uses. Sometimes, they become the art work in a room where there are no paintings or prints. When you're considering a mirror's style, look at the frame. Does it fit your redecorating scheme in terms of materials (wood, metal, or wicker)? Do its colors belong with your color scheme?

OFF TO THE MIRROR MART

There's no shortage of places to buy mirrors. They're currently the hottest item on the redecorating scene.

Depending on your style bent, check these places:

- Discount and department stores: Look in the housewares sections. They'll supply you with keep-it-simple solutions that are inexpensive, easy to hang, and easy to clean. You'll find full-length styles and a variety of vanity mirrors. You'll also find some well-framed mirrors that would look good by themselves or tucked into a grouping of pictures.

- Catalogs: Mail-order catalogs and the Internet are the easiest place to shop because you don't have to leave the house. You'll have to pay shipping costs, but you also stand to gain a quiet shopping spree in the comfort and privacy of your home. On catalog pages, you'll find more styles than you could ever hope to dream up. Specialty catalogs offer you opportunities to buy those oversize versions you'd like to have someone bring right to your door.

- Flea markets and tag and garage sales: If you have a curious decorating bent for antique, used, and not-so-used mirrors, stalk antiques sales for one-of-a-kind pieces. Anything can happen. You have a good chance of finding a bargain if you're a bargainer. It's also an opportunity to bring home a conversation starter.

Place catalog orders by phone unless they put you on hold for too long. Then, just hang up, put your order in an envelope, and mail it on your way to have cappuccino with a friend.

The Lazy Way

■ Home design stores: If you feel like leaving the house and setting out on foot just for fun, you can save shipping costs and bring home the same kinds of mirrors you see in the mail-order catalogs. You won't have as many choices as you'll find in catalogs, but you can find the newest, trendiest mirrors on the market.

YOU'VE GOT THE POWER

You can hang 'em high or lean 'em up against the wall. Incorporating mirrors into your interior scheme is one of the fastest, easiest decorating elements to handle. It's lazy style at its savviest.

Leaning Powers

Propping up mirrors in an interior is about as lazy as you can get and just as stylish. When you see how easy it is, and what the mirror can do for your room, you'll feel like you're cheating. The trick of wielding your powers of leaning is not so much a matter of knowing *how* to lean as knowing *where*.

Think big—the bigger, the better. New, used, antique, and not-so-old oversize mirrors will work light-giving wonders in a room. Here are some places to lean them:

■ Most obvious place: A full-length number leaning against a wall in a hallway will tell you how well you dressed yourself.

■ Naturally light: On a wall adjoining one with a window, a mirror will pull in more light.

IF YOU'RE SO
INCLINED

You'll easily add to the light in a narrow entry by hanging a mirror where it will catch the light of the overhead fixture or the lamp on your entryway table.

- Best view: Prop one in a corner at an angle to reflect the opposite side of the room.

- Fire in the hearth: Inside a non-working fireplace surround, a mirror will enliven an otherwise dead wall, double the sense of space in the room, and reflect the light right back at you.

- Altar image: Set a mirror on a table in a hall or stairway landing, and set a candelabra in front of it.

Making Arrangements

Re-invent the wheel, why don't we? Sometimes, lazy is just dragging the most classic, standard idea out of the archives of decorating history and doing it in a sparkling, new way. Here are three ways to lean (not hang) mirrors on the most classic of places—the mantel.

I like the idea of propping mirrors against walls or on pieces of furniture or shelves along a wall. It's comfortable to do because you don't have to make the big commitment.

If you don't have a mantel, consider making mirror arrangements on the top of a sideboard, a large trunk, or a wall-hung shelf. For any or all of these arrangements, you'll need

One to three mirrors

Glass cleaner

Paper towels

Tacky wax (a sticky clay that holds surfaces together). You can buy it in crafts supply stores

YOU'LL THANK YOURSELF LATER

It isn't easy to find a good antique mirror in good shape. It's easier to find an antique picture frame and get it fitted with a new mirror.

The Minute Mirror

1 Clean the mirror with glass cleaner and a paper towel.

2 Lean the mirror against the wall in the middle of the mantel.

3 Step back to see if you like it.

4 If you do, stop here.

5 If you think the arrangement looks too formal, pull the mirror to one side or the other.

6 Step back and decide which placement you like best.

7 Put a dot of tacky wax under the mirror frame to hold the mirror in place.

The Two-Minute Overlap

1 Collect two good-sized rectangular mirrors, one slightly larger than the other.

2 Clean the mirrors with glass cleaner and paper towels.

3 Lean the smaller mirror against the wall on the left side of the mantel.

4 Place the larger mirror on the right side of the mantel, overlapping the small mirror in the middle.

5 Stand back to check for balance.

6 Make whatever adjustments are necessary.

7 Put dots of tacky wax under the frames and press them down on the mantel or shelf.

The Double-Up

1 Collect two mantel-sized mirrors, one rectangular mirror that's larger than the other. The second mirror is a curved number—a round bull's eye mirror or an oval that can lie on its side.

2 Clean the mirror surfaces with glass cleaner and paper toweling.

3 Center the rectangular mirror in the middle of the mantel.

4 Place tacky wax under the mirror frame to keep it upright.

5 Place the curved mirror dead center in front of the rectangular mirror.

6 Tacky-wax the curved mirror in place.

YOU'LL THANK YOURSELF LATER

When arranging a group of mirrors on a mantel, don't combine a variety of frame materials. Keep frame types to a category of wood, metal, wicker, or painted frames.

QUICK ⚋ PAINLESS

Put an extra mirror tile left over (you probably bought a package of six tiles) from the dining-room table project under a footed bowl on a side table.

Optical Illusions

You can double the impact of a centerpiece on a dining-room table when you assemble a quick mirror trivet for it with beveled mirror tile. This mirror-tile trivet has an open design that doesn't take up too much space on the table, but it creates a lot of glamour and shine.

What you'll need

Five 8- or 12-inch beveled-glass mirror tiles.
White tablecloth
Dining table
Glass cleaner
Paper toweling

1 Cover your dining table with a white tablecloth.

2 Find the center of the table and place a beveled mirror tile on it. You can place it diagonally to the table's perimeter or parallel with it. (You might want to try both.) For the first arrangement, go with the parallel position.

3 Place a mirror square next to each side of the center square, butting the edges together.

4 Try this arrangement on the diagonal to see if you like it any better.

5 Choose the one you like the best and set the table.

6 Clean up any smudges you made on the tile with glass cleaner and paper towels.

7 Set your centerpiece on the tile trivet. You'll see how the image of the flower bowl (a footed one is best) is doubled and the trivet acts as its frame.

HIGH-WIRE ACT

The most common way to place mirrors is to hang them. The usual system works like picture hanging, but it's also possible to attach mirrors to walls with clips and mirror mastic, a special glue for fastening mirror glass onto flat surfaces.

These are some of the places to hang mirrors:

- Tried and true: Fasten a square or slightly rectangular mirror above a chest of drawers or vanity.

- Serviceable: Hang one on a door full-length or in a hall where you welcome guests.

- More for your money: Turn a full-length mirror on its side and hang it over the sofa to reflect more light into the room.

- Inviting: Make a small, narrow space feel more open.

- Most work: Arrange a group of small mirror squares or a collection of small decorative mirrors with beautiful frames to create the impact of one big mirror.

Five-Minute Hangings

You can swing a mirror on a hook as fast as you can hang a picture. You can hang a mirror by a wire, a sawtooth picture-hanging bar, a loop set on the center of the frame back, or by screwing the frame of the mirror right to the wall.

The wire method is the easiest way to hang a mirror. For this method, you generally need only one nail or

YOU'LL THANK YOURSELF LATER

Fastening a mirror directly to a wall is good for large, heavy mirrors or for special types, such as a round shaving mirror on an extending arm. But drilling screws through the mirror frame requires commitment. This is a good task to hire out.

hook in the wall on which to hang the mirror. Once you have the mirror hanging, it's easy to center and level out the mirror at a certain point along the wire. All you have to do is move it one way or the other on the wire and you're done.

Sawtooth bars are easy if you attach them *exactly* at the center of the frame back. The same is true for hanging loops.

Go with the laziest way, and put hanging wire on the back of your mirror frame before you hang it. For that, you'll need

Two eye screws in a size appropriate to your frame

Picture-hanging wire

Tape measure

Pencil

Small nail for starting eye-screw holes

Hammer

Wire cutter

To put a hanging wire on the back of the mirror frame,

1 Decide how you'll hang the mirror. Will it hang horizontally or vertically?

2 You will need to fasten the two eye screws that will hold the hanging wire on each side of the frame. Good points for eye screws are about three inches below the top of the frame.

3 Measure down and mark with your pencil where you'll place the eye screws.

Instead of hanging the mirror over a chest of drawers, a vanity, or a storage piece, set it on the surface of the furniture and prop it against the wall. Put your feet up, relax, and enjoy the work you did without working.

The Lazy Way

4 You'll probably need to "start" the holes for the eye screws with a nail. If that's the case, pound a small nail with your hammer at each point where an eye screw will go. Tap the nail in about a quarter inch or so and remove it.

5 Push the points of the eye screws into the started holes and tighten with your fingers. When the screws stiffen too much for you to turn them by hand, slip the nail through the eye of the screw and use it as a turning lever for further tightening.

6 Cut a length of wire. Thread the ends through the screw eyes, and twist the wire ends back on themselves to secure the wire on the back of the frame.

To hang the mirror, you'll need

Pencil

Tape measure

A picture-hanging hook with a long nail

Hammer

Someone to help you

Small carpenter's level (optional)

1 Ask someone to hold the mirror where you think you want to hang it while you stand back a distance and look at how the mirror looks in that position.

2 Go back and forth with your friend, asking him or her to change the position until you like it.

3 When you've decided, lightly mark the wall at the top of the frame with a pencil.

QUICK ⬭ PAINLESS

When small is better, the work is lighter. Choose a small mirror wiht character for a stunning focal point on a large, empty wall.

Check out what's going to be reflected in the mirror before you hang it. You wouldn't want to double the view and impact of an unsightly bookcase or cluttered cupboard.

4 Remove the mirror and ask your friend to hold the wire taut at the center.

5 Measure the length from the top of the frame to the center of the taut wire.

6 Place the end of your measure at the light mark on the wall. Measure straight down to the length you just measured on the back of the mirror and mark that spot with your pencil. That is where you'll hang your hook.

7 Pound the picture-hanging hook into the wall at the lower mark with your hammer.

8 Stand back and ask your friend to balance the mirror on its wire until it looks straight. If you're not certain about your ability to judge the mirror's level, you can always put a small level on top of the frame to check its position.

Getting Time on Your Side

	The Old Way	The Lazy Way
Hanging a mirror	Covering a whole wall with mirror tile; 5 hours	Hanging an elegant mirror by a hook; 10 minutes
Shopping for a mirror	Trips to mall; 3 hours	Shopping from home via catalogs or the Internet; 30 minutes)
Leaning a mirror	No one thought of it in the olden days; no time	Now, we're smart enough to do it in 5 minutes
Hanging a group of small mirrors	15 practice nail holes; 2 hours	Practice the arrangement on the floor first; 20 minutes
Arranging a mantel with mirrors	2 hours	15 minutes
Cleaning a mirror	10 minutes	2 minutes

Stylish Storage

Life is nothing but a mountain of Little Stuff waiting to be sorted—a gigantic collection of small necessities and not-so-necessary trinkets and souvenirs we pick up along the way. Yesterday, on my way through an airport gift shop, I noticed a small book with a big title, *Don't Sweat the Small Stuff, and It's All Small Stuff*. The words stuck to me like glue, and now I carry them around in my head.

They make me think of the Junk Drawer. You know what I mean; a house just isn't a home without one. It's that special place where you toss loose things when you don't know where else to put them. You've always aimed to eliminate the Junk Drawer—just as soon as you can get around to it.

But first, you have to do something about the bathroom closet. Every time you open the door, you can feel the pressure to reorganize (again!) all the small stuff inside—everything you need plus all that old stuff that should be thrown out such as outdated prescriptions, unused cosmetics, and that leftover first-aid equipment from the time you broke your foot.

That's not all that's bugging you. In the bedroom, the sweaters in your closet lean over the edges of shelves like

snow drifts waiting to avalanche, and when you go to sleep at night, you wonder what mysterious things are multiplying under your bed.

If you think about it for long, you can feel a sweat coming on. This is not a good thing. Sweating goes against *The Lazy Way* philosophy: Lazy people never break sweats, bend backs, or get their noses out of joint. Especially about little stuff.

THE STUFF OF LIFE

If you take an inventory of the stuff of everyday life, the list could look something like this:

In the Entry

Keys and mail

Cell phones and loose change

Purses and wallets

Planners and day runners

Hats, scarves, mittens, and gloves

Shoes and boots

Umbrellas

Coats and walking sticks

Laptops and briefcases

Clips, yellow sticky notes, and ticket stubs

In the Family Room

Tapes and CDs

Kid stuff and cat toys

Books and magazines

Family albums and photos

Newspapers and trade pieces

Funniest family videos and popcorn bowls

Games and toys

The TV schedule

In the Dining Room

Glassware and crystal

Candlesticks

Decanters

Trays and table linens

China and silver

Wedding gifts you hate but can't throw out

In the Kitchen

Spices and condiments

Flatware and kitchen tools

Napkins and dishtowels

Rags and wipe-ups

Cookie cutters

Dishes and glasses

Pots, pans, and food supplies

Baking supplies

Clean-up tools

In the Office

Pens and pencils

Clips and rubberbands

YOU'LL THANK YOURSELF LATER

Assemble a small tray or basket beside the phone to keep pens and note pads handy for messages.

Rulers and straight edges

Bills

Tax files you're avoiding

Stationery and stamps

Pins and tacks

Computer discs

Stapler, staples, and tapes

Paper supplies

In the Bedroom

Water glasses

Reading glasses

Tissues

Books and magazines

Sleeping masks and cuddly wraps

Socks and shoes

Ties, scarves, and jewelry

Sweaters and jeans

Skirts, shirts, and slacks

Pillows and blankets

A trail of laundry

In the Bath

Soaps and bath salts

Shower supplies

Lotions and cosmetics

Eye-care needs

Toothbrushes

Drugs and prescriptions

Candles and soap dishes

Tubes of toothpaste, combs, and hair brushes

First-aid supplies

Towels and linens

Heating pads and aspirins

Cleaning supplies

Hair products and hair dryers

The Kids' Rooms

Don't go there.

Sweating seems like the appropriate thing to do. A horrible thought crosses your mind: Little Stuff could be your Life's Work.

Okay, that's it. We're drawing the line. Little Stuff is just little stuff waiting to be sorted. It's time for the wisdom of lazy.

DON'T BREAK DOWN: BREAK IT DOWN

Don't surrender to clutter. Meet the challenge head-on so you'll be able to sit back and relax in comfort and peace. In the same way that you meet the overwhelming prospect of redecorating your entire home by breaking it down into small increments, take on an oversized load of clutter. One small step at a time will do it.

QUICK  PAINLESS

Take five minutes (set the timer) to make a list of storage problems in your house. Just listing them gets you closer to resolving them.

To make the subject of storage easy, I've categorized it into three main clutter-busting groups of containers.

- Closets, cupboards, and furniture pieces (as in dressers, chests of drawers, wardrobes, linen presses, armoires, stacking drawers, blanket chests, dining-room sideboards, pie safes, highboys, and china cabinets)

- Racks and pegs, stands, and shelves (such as wall-hung open shelves, standing bookcases, plate and pie stands, baker's racks, and Shakers' pegs)

- Boxes, baskets, and bins (which translates into wooden bowls, trays, tool and apple boxes, old leather suitcases, wicker containers with lids, handles, and open tops, trunks, galvanized metal boxes and chests, plastic units molded for everything from flatware to laundry, wire carriers, terra cotta pots, and great, white porcelain bowls)

I briefly discuss the big-storage closet and cupboards, but I'd like to spend more time with the clutter-cutters out in full view that have a lot to do with shaping up the redecorated look of a room. They're also the easier, lazier, and much more rewarding things you can add to your home.

BEHIND CLOSED DOORS

Most homes have closets and kitchen cupboards for food staples, clothing, and bedding. They're the "little rooms" of your house where you put away what you don't want running around loose. They give you an orderly place to go for your daily and weekly needs.

When you don't have enough closets and cupboards, you search for furniture pieces to flesh out your storage needs. It's easy to find and buy typical furniture storage, but sometimes, "thinking outside the box" will gain you surprising and welcome storage in places you never thought of before. Here's what I mean:

- Instead of a beside-the-chair table to hold your reading lamp in the family room, use a small chest of drawers. You can stash away the little stuff where it's within easy reach without getting up and going to a closet.

- Add a settee or bench to the foot of your bed to catch that stack of decorative bed pillows when you crawl in for the night.

- Stack old leather suitcases or wicker trunks to make a bedside table. This is an especially good idea for small-space apartments.

- Use the space under the coffee table for stacking magazines and books, games, and baskets of CDs, and videotapes.

- In a small dining room, substitute a chest of drawers for a large sideboard or highboy.

- Paint a wooden outdoor serving cart to use indoors as a bedside stand.

QUICK ☜🐭☞ PAINLESS

The place for ditsy little baskets is inside drawers and out of sight where they can keep the smallest items in line. Too many little (even well-organized) containers out in a room has the look of clutter.

Quick-Serve Cupboard

Here's The Lazy Way *wisdom at work: A kitchen cupboard with convenience-store smarts that's set up to serve passers-by with a variety of instant drinks and condiments. This idea also finds a home for all those leftover fast-food condiment packets you seem to collect. Once you've organized the cupboard, you can serve the kids without lifting a finger; they'll serve themselves. When friends hang out in your kitchen while you cook, you can open the doors and say, "Help yourselves!"*

To organize your quick-serve unit, you'll need

Clear drinking glasses or low, wide bowls for single-serve cream, sugar, salt, pepper, ketchup, jam, soy sauce, mustard, relish, coffee, tea, cider, and hot chocolate packets

Small wire bin for stir-sticks, spoons, and chopsticks

Clear glass or plastic containers with lids to store supplies of croutons, crackers, cookies, and candy

1 Organize the packets in the clear glass bowls and drinking glasses, fitting the packet sizes to the containers.

2 Fill the lidded see-through containers with cookies, crackers, candy, and whatever else you would like to make handy for guests.

3 Stand stir-sticks, chopsticks, and spoons in a wire basket or in tall glasses.

4 Arrange the taller items toward the back of the cupboard and the shorter ones in front.

When you finish your quick-serve cupboard in the kitchen, sit back and watch how well it works. You might be tempted to make mental notes for improvements, but you don't have to do anything about it at the moment.

The Lazy Way

Office in a Box

When I was on a magazine scouting trip to San Francisco one spring, a homeowner showed me her compact home office inside a tiny box of a house overlooking the water. She said she and her husband were "house-poor" from buying the expensive home on the Bay, but the fabulous view had been worth it.

Meanwhile, she needed a home office for her work to help pay for that view. In her living room, just inside the front door of the cottage, she placed a tall armoire. In a short time, she was plugged in, writing her stories and catching the view between jobs.

Here's what you need to create a box office of your own:

Armoire, wardrobe, or cupboard with adjustable shelves, drawers, and doors

Computer and accessories

Office supplies

Baskets and office boxes to hold supplies

Small table (work surface) borrowed from the room where the armoire stands

Chair

If necessary, cut a hole in the back of the armoire to thread electrical cords to the socket. You can do this with an electric drill, driver, or saw kit:

1 First, drill a large-sized hole to give the saw a place to begin. Then, cut a small hole to allow the computer plug-in to go through the armoire back.

2 Move the armoire to its place on the wall.

YOU'LL THANK YOURSELF LATER

When selecting baskets or office boxes, gather containers with similar surfaces. That way, if sizes or patterns vary, the containers' common textures will be a unifying element.

Try a short stool as a stand. On it, set a rectangular basket to hold books, newspapers, or bath towels. You'll love this stand's portability.

3 Set in the computer power pack and store the monitor on an eye-level shelf (eye level when you're seated). Stash the keyboard on a shelf.

4 Arrange your office supplies in don't-we-look-good-together trays, baskets, and bins.

When you're working, pull a table from the room close to the armoire and place the keyboard on the table. Slide a chair in to the work surface. When you're finished working, tuck away the keyboard and papers, return the table and chair to their original places in the room, and close the office doors.

INSTANT REDECORATING: FAST RACK, QUICK PEG, EASY STAND, OR OPEN SHELF

Part of any lazy decorating caper is to kill two birds with one stone. While you're organizing your small stuff, you're also redecorating your home.

Whenever you're racking up or hanging things on pegs, use practical possessions and useful collections as decorative material. Try these out-in-the-open ideas:

- Hang a collection of hats, umbrellas, and walking sticks on pegs in an entrance or hallway. (Keep the ugly-but-favorite hats hidden in the closet so they don't ruin the display.)

- Hang baskets on hooks to collect gloves, keys, and other small objects left on every available surface whenever someone comes home. Assign a basket to each member of the household.

- If you have a handsome pot-and-pan collection, hang them from "S" hooks fastened on metal bars in the kitchen.

- Use wall hooks for bath towels and robes.

- To bring your outdated kitchen into the next century, remove a few doors to reveal the shelves inside. Freshen with paint and display your dishes on your new easy-reach cupboard shelves.

Beauty and the Bath

The payback for reorganizing this room is a bath that gives you the pristine comforts of a private spa in a luxury hotel.

You'll need

Three-tiered stand with shelves or baskets

Small basket

Pure, white bars of soap

Bathtub valet

Wall hooks

Screwdriver

Tub-side bench

Candles and matches

Bubble bath

Thirsty white towels

Natural sponges (optional)

White terrycloth robes

A COMPLETE WASTE OF TIME

The 3 Worst Ways to Handle Storage:

1. Ignore the container as decorative potential in a room.

2. Hang on to things someone else could use.

3. Let the stuff pile up.

1 Arrange newly laundered towels in the three-tiered stand and tuck in a small basket of extra soaps, candles, and sponges.

2 Fasten wall hooks on the wall with a screwdriver for robes and wet towels.

3 Lay the bathtub valet across the tub and set it up with candles, soap, and a sponge. You'll need matches, too.

4 Place the bench near the tub and use it to sit on before and after your bath.

Now, for the relaxing part: Wrap yourself in a robe and run a tub of hot water filled with bubbles....

At Your Service

Storage and display pieces are important for a well-functioning dining room. If you're in a small dining room, or if you can't yet afford the highboy or hutch you want, fill in with an open-shelved cart and a wooden bench that hugs the wall. To pull together dining room storage that serves you well, you'll need

Three-tiered serving cart

Wooden bench

Plate stands

Shoebox-sized wicker baskets

Dishes

Table linens

Serving pieces

Glassware

Flatware

When you finish Beauty and the Bath, light the candles and turn off the bathroom lights. Sink into the water up to your neck, close your eyes, and think about how good you feel. Open your eyes to see how great your body looks in the candlelight. Take a trip in your mind, and don't come back until you're ready.

The Lazy Way

1. Use your dining room tabletop for display and storage between meals. Keep a plate stand on the table at all times as if it were a centerpiece, setting it just to one side of the center of the table. On the plate stand, keep a supply of clean dishes ready for use.

2. Spread clean linens on the shelves of the serving cart and arrange your glassware (lip side down) on a lower shelf. Arrange your large serving pieces on the top shelf of the serving cart.

3. Line the baskets with napkins. In one basket, stow away your flatware. In another, arrange stacks of napkins. Fill a third with napkin rings, a fourth with serving spoons. Leave one empty for serving dinner rolls.

4. Along the length of the wooden bench near the serving cart, line up the matching baskets.

HASSLE-FREE STORAGE: BOXES, BASKETS, AND BINS

For really easy storage, round up an inventory of cool baskets, boxes, and bins that make strong decorating statements and fit your decorating scheme. Choose bigger containers rather than ditsy little ones. Plan to arrange your smallest trays and baskets inside larger ones. For example, when you sort clips, rubberbands, and other tiny office paraphernalia, arrange them in small baskets that suit their size. Then, arrange the small baskets in a larger tray to keep them from getting scattered around on the desktop or in a drawer. By storing small containers inside larger ones, you stay organized and simplify the look of your rooms.

Check out this list of storage ideas you can create with boxes, baskets, and bins:

- Place a tall container on the kitchen counter for your favorite kitchen tools.

- Arrange loose photos, snapshots, and cards you want to keep handy in a wicker basket with dividers.

- Keep bills in a special container just their size and tuck it into a drawer.

- Ask an old-fashioned tool box to play valet at your breakfast table. Fill it with napkins, flatware, salt-and-pepper shakers and whatever else you need for table service. Tuck in a vase of wildflowers from time to time.

- Stow CDs and cassette tapes inside lidded wicker baskets that slide under the coffee table or into a cabinet.

- In great, wide bowls, store colorful and appetizing fruits and vegetables out in the open.

- Use plate-drying racks to display everyday dishes.

- Organize small book collections in baskets or bins to line up on your coffee table—all within easy reach.

QUICK ⬭ PAINLESS

For your dining room display, use your napkins as decorative elements by fluffing them out like flowers in your crystal or water glasses.

Welcome Back, Warrior

Nothing feels better after a day away at battle than to come home to an entry that says, "Hi, how was your day? May I take your things off your hands?" Here's what you'll need to make coming home a special occasion:

Hall or entry table with shelves

Mirror

Large wooden or wicker tray for catching keys, loose change, and pocket contents

Mail rack

1 Place the table inside the entry.

2 Hang or lean a mirror on the table surface.

3 Arrange the tray and the mail rack on the tabletop.

4 Keep the shelf or shelves under the hall table clear of little stuff that may find its way there. Tell everyone in the house that the shelves are for purses, laptops, briefcases, and leaving-the-house needs.

A COMPLETE WASTE OF TIME

The 3 Worst Ways to Choose a Storage Container:

1. Choose the wrong container for the task.

2. Choose a container not in keeping with its surroundings.

3. Ignore the need for a storage container.

Easy Bedside Manners

Ah, another chance for a personal (and very lazy) reward. You can make this storage project as luxurious and languid as your newly organized bath if you begin with a bedside table that has drawers. Use a small set of drawers for your bedside table. If you must use a table with legs, arrange a basket or small trunk for storage in the space underneath it.

Nothing matches slipping between the sheets of a newly made bed and sliding down into the comforts of a comforter. Every time you do this, thank yourself for making your bedside manner more refined.

The Lazy Way

What you'll need includes

Small chest of drawers or a table with drawers

Bedside reading lamp

A tray or charger to collect small items you need to keep close at hand

Personal bedside needs and wants

Clock, radio, or a combination of both

Freshly laundered sheets and pillowcases

A fluffy new duvet or comforter

1 Begin with the lamp as the table's predominant decorative item. Place it where you can comfortably read by it.

2 Arrange the next largest items so you can see them from your bed.

3 Add the tray for your personal treasures and arrange them on the tray.

4 Slide the less attractive items inside your table's drawers.

5 Make up the bed with your new linens and climb in.

Getting Time on Your Side

	The Old Way	The Lazy Way
The small stuff	Ignore it until you're swimming in it.	Take on the small stuff one low-strain step at a time.
Food supplies	Keep them in their original store wrappers so you can riffle through them in search of something to eat.	Take the pressure off the hunt for food with a few see-through lidded storage. containers.
Phone messages	Forget to pass on a phone message because you can't remember the number or the name and can't find paper to write it.	Write the message on the wall. It's the least you can do.
When you come home	Scatter your possessions in a trail through the house.	Pause for one minute inside the house and return your possessions to their allotted places by the door.
Soap and towels	Don't provide a soap dish or drying bars for towels.	Corral bath needs on great looking storage.

Chapter fourteen

Ten-Minute Flower Arranging

You'll love *The Lazy Way* of flower arranging: The less work you put into arranging flowers, the better they'll look. In other words, if you let flowers be what they naturally want to be instead of torturing them into unlikely, distorted arrangements, you'll save time and they'll look their best.

I don't think I've ever spent more than five minutes assembling a bouquet. It's probably because I'm impatient, pressed for time, or have some kind of attention deficit disorder. Oddly enough, the flowers don't seem to mind, and thanks to their endless beauty and bounty, I can always come up with something wonderful.

It's a matter of backing off and listening. Flowers have a way of speaking gently and calmly to you, making subtle and easy suggestions for how they want you to handle them and which vase suits them best. The spirit of lazy-style falls right in with their easy charms.

LAZY RULES FOR FLOWER ARRANGING

Whenever you prepare to arrange a few flowers, keep these relaxed rules of arranging in mind:

Lazy rule #1: Treat flowers as you'd like to be treated. (Sounds like the Golden Rule, doesn't it?) When you bring them home from the flower market, be sure they're wrapped so they're protected from cold winter winds or drying heat. When you get them home, remove most of the foliage from their stems and make fresh cuts on the ends of their stems so they can drink more freely. Then, immerse the stems in a bucket of warm water and put the bucket in a cool location until you're ready to make your flower arrangement.

Lazy rule #2: Don't force flowers into unwieldy shapes. Let them tell you (by their natural growth) which container they want. For example, short-stemmed, bushy flowers suggest wide, generous containers. Tall, slender-stemmed flowers beg for tall, simple cylinders that will show off their architecture.

Lazy rule #3: There are no hard-and-fast rules about which flowers go in which vase. Common sense tells you that any type of flower can be treated to a casual container for an informal look or given a dressier vase for a more formal occasion.

Lazy rule #4: Use only one type of flower per vase. Mixing and matching flowers in the same vase is

A COMPLETE WASTE OF TIME

The 3 Worst Things to Do When Arranging Flowers:

1. Transport them unprotected in freezing weather.

2. Forget to put them in water when you get them home from the flower market.

3. Cut their stems too short.

time-consuming and complicated and doesn't look any more wonderful than a simply glorious mass of the same kind of flowers.

THE VASES OF EASE

Lazy vases can be anything that holds water and keeps flowers standing almost upright. Here's a brief run-down of six types of containers you can consider and collect for stress-free flower arranging.

| Bud vase | Cylinder | Urn | Bucket | Bowl | Box |

Types of Vases.

This Bud's for You

The classic bud vase with its slender, curved body has one standout characteristic that makes it different from most other vases: A narrow neck. The bud vase's neck and slim body limit the number of blooms it can hold. It's the first vase out of a florist shop every day because it's so quick-and-easy to fill. It also doesn't cost much to create an arrangement in one.

You can find bud vases in the most unexpected places. You'll recognize them by their slender bodies and narrow tops:

- Bud vases (available in craft, florist, and home stores, antiques shops, and supermarkets)
- Wine, vinegar, and olive oil bottles
- Soda (that's pronounced "pop" in the west, "coke" in the south) bottles
- Antique glass milk bottles
- Chemistry bottles and old medicine bottles
- Wine carafes

Say It with Cylinders

A cylindrical vase might be as slim and round as a bud vase or as wide and boxy as a brown-paper lunch bag. You'll recognize it by its characteristic straight up-and-down, distinctly contemporary body. It has no flirty curves or shapes, and its wide-open top is as big as its bottom. Keep a decorating eye out for these stately looking cylinders:

- Tall and short drinking glasses
- Curved or rectangular cylindrical vases (look in art and museum stores for the most elegant ones)
- Tall, narrow paper bags (lined with plastic)
- Bar ware
- Pitchers
- Champagne coolers and ice chests
- Soup pots
- Watering cans

Urn Your Flower-Arranging Skills

Nothing matches the classic Greek amphora urn for easy flower arranging. Its generous, circular body invites the stems to spread and lean inside the container, and its narrow neck collects the blooms together at the top, practically arranging them for you. The following list is short, but a supply of these classic urns will get you rave reviews whenever it comes to flower arranging.

- Classic white or glass urn-shaped vases
- Ironstone pitchers

Bucket Brigade

Put out the flowers in bucket-shaped vases. You have many bucket-style containers in your house right now. More are waiting out there. Start with this list of containers that are wider at the top than they are at the bottom:

- Classic wide-necked urns on pedestals
- Drinking glasses and coffee mugs with flared tops
- Stemware
- Garden pots
- Apple baskets (lined)
- Metal florist's tins
- Flared pitchers
- Crocks
- Galvanized buckets and pails

YOU'LL THANK YOURSELF LATER

Keep a collection of vases within easy reach to avoid the hassle of trying to find something suitable when flowers suddenly appear at your doorstep.

Bowl 'Em Over

Shallow and wide, the bowl is another one of the most available flower containers you have in your house. They're in your kitchen cupboards waiting for a decorating whim to come along. Consider these containers the next time you feel like tossing together a dinner table centerpiece:

- Soup tureens
- Serving bowls
- Breadbaskets
- Large salad bowls
- Mixing bowls

Box 'Em Up

You probably don't think of boxes as vases, but they're excellent for one reason or another.

A box or box-shaped basket can contain a number of small flower vases to create a large, unified mass of flowers. A box can hide a not-so-attractive glass vase that doesn't fit into a setting. Seeing flowers pop out of a box or paper bag is an element of surprise worth creating.

Start with the boxy containers listed below and add a few of your own:

- Crates
- Berry boxes
- Trays
- Baskets

QUICK 〈🐷〉 *PAINLESS*

Pick up a supply of marbles or decorative stones to put in the bottoms of vases. It might be necessary to weight wide-topped vases with bouquets that are taller and wider than their containers.

- Antique milk carriers with bottles
- Metal bins

The container or vase you choose is the key to a successful 10-minute arrangement. The only way to learn what works is to practice arranging flowers in a variety of containers. Start small, repeat your successes, and before you know it you'll be arranging flowers in no time without even thinking about it.

FAST-FORWARD FLOWERS

When you're pressed for time, there's nothing like flowers to cover all the bases: They'll cheer up a weary room, make an occasion special, and put a new spin on your outlook. They add color to dull spaces, elements of surprise in a hum-drum world, and beauty and romance wherever they go.

Lazy arranging is largely dependent on the container you choose for your flowers. On the following pages, you'll find recipes for creating bouquets in a variety of containers: Bud vases, cylinders, bowls, buckets, baskets, and urns. Each project suggests a place or home site where the arrangement will work best.

YOU'LL THANK YOURSELF LATER

The next time you're in a craft or floral shop, buy a block or two of floral foam (sometimes known as an *oasis*) to keep on hand. It'll save you the time it takes to run out for it later.

QUICK 〰 PAINLESS

Single and Loving It

A single, perfect bloom standing in a tall, elegant piece of stemware will be the star attraction on your midnight buffet. Tuck it in among your best crystal and stemware glasses so your guests can admire it as they serve themselves.

You'll need

A tall, slender stemware glass

Cool water

One perfect, distinctive flower such as a rose, peony, or lily

Flower clipper

1. Fill the stemware glass with water to within an inch or two of the lip.

2. Strip away excess leaves on the stem so that only a few good ones remain.

3. Cut the end of the stem to fit the vase. (To gauge where you'll want to cut it, place it next to the glass on the outside.)

4. Settle the flower into the water so that its face is directed toward your guests.

Rose Parade

The days of wine and formally arranged roses are past. At $3 a pop, a dozen long-stemmed roses squandered in a single vase is as rare as a flight to the moon. Here's a way to cut the actual number of blooms in half and still have a dozen roses: Arrange them in slender containers on a mantel, shelf, or table in front of a mirror. The mirror will reflect them and double their number.

To create a parade of roses, you'll need

Five cylinder and bud-vase containers that look good
together (four drinking glasses and a curved chemistry
vial or a bud vase)

Warm water

Six roses

Clippers

Display ledge, shelf, or tabletop with a mirror

1 Arrange the containers on the ledge in front of the mirror.

2 Fill the containers with water.

3 Remove extra foliage from the roses' stems so that only a few good leaves remain close to each flower.

4 Arrange the roses tentatively in the containers so you can decide just how much to cut off each stem. Make one rose taller than the others and two or three a little shorter, and lean the last two over the edges of their containers. One container will hold two blooms.

5 Trim the stems to the length you like. Give the ends a vertical cut to open the stem to the water a little further.

Rose Bowl

Use six roses in a small compote, crowding them close togeth-er for impact. This is an especially effective mood-maker on a small, private dinner table. Add a candle or two, and you're set for a wonderful time with someone you love.

You'll need

A piece of stemware with a generous, flared-out bowl
Six perfect roses
Six short (about six inches long) lemon-leaf branches
Warm water
Clippers

1 Fill the stemware with water.

2 Pull the leaves off the rose stems and clip the stems to about four inches (depending on the size of the container).

3 Arrange the roses in a clump in the center of the bowl.

4 Tuck short branches of lemon leaves around the perimeter of the bowl, completely encircling the flowers.

5 Trim away excess length on stems if necessary and rearrange.

IF YOU'RE SO
INCLINED

Combine the rose parade idea with the rose bowl idea and make a parade of rose bowls in a line down the center of your dining room table (that is, if you have a lot of gar-den roses you can pick for free).

Back-Lot or Ditch-Weed Arrangement

Don't overlook ditches and back lots for floral material. Some of the most wonderful grasses and weeds can be picked for free and slipped into household containers to brighten a room. I like to gather a series of great-looking, used-up olive oil, wine, and vinegar bottles to act as bud vases for weed and wildflower specimens that catch my eye.

For back-lot flower arranging, you'll need

Seven graceful wine, oil, and vinegar bottles

A variety of non-wilting, back-lot weeds, grasses, and wild-flowers

Cool water

Kitchen shears

1 Fill the bottles with water.

2 Slip a single stem or two into each bottle, clipping their stems as necessary.

3 Arrange the bottles together on a table.

YOU'LL THANK YOURSELF LATER

Don't pick weeds and flowers in preserved areas or parks. Confine your weed cutting to ditches and back lots that aren't protected by law.

Pitcher Perfect

In your repertoire of vases, be sure you have a large, classic white ironstone pitcher or a large white pitcher that has the look of ironstone. A group of ironstone pitchers is even better. Having a group of white pitchers gives you flexibility with the sizes and types of flowers you can display and combine.

I found my favorite ironstone flower-arranging pitcher at a rural antiques store for $5—a major coup for true ironstone. The owner of the store apologized for the fact that the pouring lip was cracked. It didn't bother me! I liked the price, and the beautiful urn-like shape of the pitcher was one spectacular flower vase in the making. Years later, it still stands on a white ceramic counter near my kitchen window, displaying a progression of dramatic seasonal blooms: Apple-tree branches with blossoms, graceful arcs of lilac and peony branches, and May bridal wreath from my neighbor's shrub. Summer and fall provide mustard, dill weed, daisies, and huge hydrangea blooms that stay and stay and stay. By the end of the year, my pitcher holds evergreen branches, supermarket specials, and a subtle combination of air-freshening eucalyptus and baby's breath.

For pitcher arranging, you'll need

White pitcher
Flowers of a suitable size for the pitcher
Water
Clippers or kitchen shears

QUICK ⬤ PAINLESS

Good places to find white pitchers for flower arranging: antiques shops, housewares departments in large department or discount stores, flea and mail-order

1 Fill the pitcher with water.

2 Pull away excess leaves from the flower stems and make fresh cuts on the bottoms of the stems so the flowers will take in more water.

3 One at a time, set branches or stems inside the pitcher, leaning the most dramatic and curvaceous branches across the pitcher lip. Vary the height of the branches.

4 Trim branches or stems that are too long.

5 Change the water every two or three days.

IF YOU'RE SO
INCLINED

In the winter just before the trees leaf out, celebrate the season with a stand of flowering tree branches in a tall white vase or pitcher.

Water Garden

The element of water is an essential part of flower arranging that's usually invisible. Unless your container is glass, you miss it. A large salad bowl filled with water, stones, and a flower head or two is one way to enjoy this fluid, life-giving element.

For a water garden, you'll need

A large, broad salad bowl (preferably glass or white porcelain)

Water

Decorative stones

Two floating candles

Long-nosed lighter

One perfect gardenia or rose bloom

1 Fill the salad bowl with water.

2 Arrange decorative stones in the bottom of the bowl.

3 Float the candles on the water.

4 Add the flower bloom.

5 Light the candles.

Milk Carrier Showcase

An antique milk carrier illustrates how you can combine several small vases inside a large container to make an impact with only a few flower stems. Glass milk bottles inside the carrier serve as bud vases that will keep floppy flowers, such as daisies and wild grasses, standing upright. If you can't find an antique milk carrier or its corresponding set of glass milk bottles, you can substitute a boxy wicker basket and a set of empty wine carafes. Try it with a soda crate and soda bottles or a wine rack and empty wine bottles. Empty jelly jars in an old utensil tray could work, too.

To corral summer's bounty in a group arrangement, you'll need

Milk carrier, soda carton, or wine rack with empty bottles
Water
Daisies and wild grasses
Kitchen shears

1 Fill the glass bottles with water.

2 Hold a flower stem against the bottle to measure how much you'll cut off to make the flower the right height in the vase. (In this arrangement, the flower heads look best standing only four or five inches above the neck of the bottle.)

3 Cut stems and insert the flowers into the vases.

4 Cut and arrange the grasses to stand inside the vases with the flowers.

Low Bowler

Sometimes, a bowl arrangement is so low that it requires built-in bottoms-up support for the flowers. This is because the container has no sides to keep the flowers upright. For a low, wide-open arrangement, you can use floral foam, or oasis, to keep your flowers in place. Floral foam is a block of green material that, when soaked in water, becomes heavy. The foam block is soft enough to poke stems into it yet firm enough to keep the stems in place. Here's a bowl arrangement that works well at a dinner table because the arrangement is low enough for diners to see over it. You'll need

Shallow bowl (in or on a stand is especially nice)

Water

Floral foam

Butter knife

Short-stemmed blossoms

Kitchen shears

QUICK ✦ PAINLESS

When you're creating a shallow bowl arrangement, you can add elegance by creating a stand or "foot" for it. Just invert another shallow bowl of the same color and place it under the bottom of the vase.

1 Place the floral foam inside the bowl vase to estimate how much foam you'll need to cut away to set it firmly inside the bowl.

2 Cut away excess foam with the butter knife until it fits snugly in the container.

3 Soak the floral foam in water for 30 minutes.

4 Insert the short-stemmed flowers into the foam in a fairly even mound over the bowl.

Paper Bag Vase

It's tempting to go outside the usual flower containers when you see the array of paper bags available for gift wrap. Brown-paper lunch bags are always great (and you always have a few in the house), but some of the shiny-coated gift bags (especially white ones) make fun and unexpected vases.

All you need is a waterproof vase that will fit inside the bag out of sight while it keeps your bouquet in water. Try this bag-waterproofing solution: Place a plastic food storage bag around a bouquet. Add a little water and tie a string around the top of the bag and flower stems before setting it inside the paper bag.

For this paper-bag vase, you'll need

Decorative paper bag

Plastic food storage bag or glass vase that fits inside the paper bag

Supermarket flowers

Water

Kitchen shears

1 Fill the glass vase with water.

2 Set the vase inside the paper bag.

3 Arrange the flowers inside the vase, cutting the stems as needed with the kitchen shears.

Ever Green

In the dead of winter, don't stop arranging flowers. Their presence will remind you of the returning summer sun and keep you from feeling dried up and dormant—especially if you remember the evergreens.

When everything else has gone underground, evergreens tell you there's still life on the planet. In winter at my house, they replace the summer flower display I keep outside my front door. Out where there's snow, I don't water them, and in March, they're as fresh as the day I bought them from the Christmas tree lot in November.

To assemble an evergreen bouquet to keep in or out of the house, you'll need

Fresh-cut evergreen branches

Bare shrubbery twigs (preferably red)

A wide-mouthed urn on a pedestal or a plain country bucket

Clippers

1 Tentatively arrange the evergreen branches in the urn.

2 Remove them one at a time to trim them to the right lengths with your clippers.

3 Re-insert the branches in the urn.

4 Add sprigs of bare branches for contrast.

Getting Time on Your Side

	The Old Way	The Lazy Way
Arranging a basket bouquet	30 minutes	10 minutes
Arranging a bouquet in a garden urn	30 minutes	10 minutes
Arranging a dozen roses	30 minutes	10 minutes
Arranging a bud vase	10 minutes	5 minutes
Arranging a tabletop centerpiece	1 hour	With floral foam, 15 minutes

Candle Power

Yeah, I know; you'll think I'm lying when I tell you this, but it's the honest truth: I had a grandmother who lived by candlelight in a sod-house shanty on a North Dakota prairie. What's a sod-house shanty? A house carved out of a hillside and roofed over with sod—that's grass. Sort of like the earth dwellings hippies built in the 60s.

My grandmother's legacy is one of those Depression stories, the kind you want to walk away from when the old folks start telling you how hard life was "back then." But there's something poignant and positive about the image I have of her sitting by the fire in a pool of candlelight, stitching a pretty pillow for her home—a small act of defiance to defeat the darkness and the cold.

We might not live in sod huts, but we experience hardships as heavy as my grandmother's: We're too busy for our own good, drowning in an overload of information, our lives complicated by speed and a need for psychological endurance. This chapter is about small acts of defiance you can carry out to take the hard edges off your life.

Take a breather. Curl up with a kitty, and light a candle to soften the night. The story goes something like this.

WHEN YOU'RE BURNING THE CANDLE AT BOTH ENDS

If your time seems to dissolve and you don't feel you're getting anything done, which of course makes you feel stressed out and guilty, stop. You could do something (something close to nothing) that would relax you and probably shed some new light on things.

"Something close to nothing" is another phrase for lighting a candle. Nothing makes a room more wonderful with less effort than candlelight. It's lazy decorating at its peak. All you need is a match, a candle, something to set your candle in, and a bit of time to appreciate the elegant attitude-changing light.

I scope out the multitude of candles and candle holders you can choose from in a minute. First, I'd like to list the benefits (what you gain for spending little money and for doing practically nothing) of candlelight at home.

- You look better in a room lit by candlelight. It flatters your skin tones and hides little flaws you'd like to eliminate.

- Your rooms look better by candlelight. No one sees its small deformities, big flaws, or dust balls.

- Candlelight creates illusions about what might be the real world. At least, the world *seems* gentler and kinder under the glow of a candle or two.

A COMPLETE WASTE OF TIME

The 3 Worst Things to Do with a Candle:

1. Set it directly on a piece of furniture.

2. Leave it unattended in the room.

3. Burn a scented candle at the dinner table.

- A bath by candlelight puts a new cast on things—your body and your mood.

- Citronella candles on a balcony or deck might keep insects at bay. If they're not successful, they will still put an energizing mood on an evening outdoors.

- Candles in candlesticks highlight a focal point in a room, exaggerating textures and shapes that vanish in the daylight.

- Candles combined with flowers make a killer team for creating romance and intimacy in a room.

With their flickering and fanning, candle flames raise a room's emotional temperature and excitement level. They add movement and energy to your sensibilities while you sit in the shadows of their fire. It doesn't get any better.

CANDLES TO LIGHT AT ONE END

Here's a rundown of candle types you can use to quickly bring on the redecorating benefits. I haven't listed sculptural candles or candles of color because they tend to complicate situations by burning down in unusual ways or spilling colorful stains where you don't want them. For lazy purposes, I'm limiting the list to the *simplest* ways to light up your nights. Here are the stress-free, low-maintenance candles to buy:

- Tapers: Narrower at the top than they are at the bottom, tapers are the first candles ever made and the first shape that comes to mind with the word candle.

YOU'LL THANK YOURSELF LATER

Store candles in a cool, dry, dark place. Wrap them in aluminum foil and put them in a refrigerator or freezer for a few hours before using them. The extra cold is said to slow down their burning.

▨ Church and synagogue candles: Sturdy, stately white columns are the lights of religious rites. Their widths range from half-inch diameters to two and three inches, and their sides are straight up and down.

▨ Floating candles: Any candle will float if it's given enough water, but floating candles are made conveniently small for floating on small amounts of water. These rounded dollops of wax with wicks measure about $1\frac{1}{2}$ inches across.

▨ Pillars: Straight up and down like columns, pillars vary in thickness from 2-inch to 8- and 10-inch diameters. Height-wise, pillars never go much over 12 inches—stocky versions of the church candle. Thicker pillars have as many as five wicks.

▨ Beeswax candles: Another early type of candle, they're made from the wax created by bees. Once the wax is harvested from the beehive, it's cut into squares and rolled around lengths of candle wicking into narrow columns for burning.

▨ Tea lights: These tiny candles originally kept tea and casseroles warm in their servers. In the 70s, they were popular in fondue servers. Now, we treat them as decorative votive candles. Buy the ones with tin or plastic wraps.

▨ Votive candles: My computer says "votives" is not a word. However, it'll accept "votive candle." Doesn't it know that everyone uses the shorter word and you see it everywhere on candle labels? "Votive" is popularly applied to a small candle in a container that's lit for special occasions. It originated in early church customs where small candles were burned with prayers and wishes for others at votive masses.

Most candles are freestanding (not hidden inside a holder). Others, such as votive candles, are completely contained by their holder.

Advantages of one over the other? It's a toss-up. Freestanding candles, if they're not of the dripless variety, can drip down the sides of the candle to the holder. Sometimes, it's a desirable look that takes you back in time. At other times, wax drips are a nuisance and a disappointment when they spill onto good linens or wood finishes.

Candles that are completely contained (and, occasionally, wide pillars) can build up a pool of wax and drown the wick and the flame. Generally, you get what you pay for in wax. A more expensive candle will burn without melting down too quickly. Check the labels and packaging, and ask the store clerk what you can expect from your candle purchase.

QUICK-AND-EASY CANDLE HOLDERS

Lazy-style candle holders have a lot in common with lazy-style flower vases. Both are pulled together from everyday dishes and containers, even though there are plenty of official candlesticks and flowerpots around. Part of *The Lazy Way* is a relaxation of rules for using the "correct" container. Both types of containers—candleholders and vases—hold and display the most magical elements of redecorating and can be arranged in many of the

YOU'LL THANK YOURSELF LATER

Keep a supply of candles on hand in case an occasion comes up, the electricity goes off, or you're suddenly hit by a redecorating mood. It could happen.

same ways: In lines or groupings, as singles, or as twin components. Sometimes, you can use the same container to hold either candles or flowers. For example, use a favorite flower urn to hold a giant pillar candle.

Put your candles in these different containers:

- Sconces: Wall-hung brackets will hold one or more candles each and usually hang on a hook like a picture. The more interesting ones are available in antiques shops, but you can also find them in contemporary housewares departments. You can choose from brass, silver, wrought iron, punched tin, and pewter.

- Candlesticks: Grossly available at all sorts of prices, you can have candlesticks in wood, silver, glass, crystal, iron, and tin. They're luxury items you buy for yourself or give to others as gifts.

- Candle pots: Anything that welcomes a small votive candle is a candle pot. This super-popular category encourages you to see candle holders in all sorts of things—terra cotta pots; glass cups; carved-out oranges, apples, and pumpkins; and all sorts of ceramic bowls.

- Candle stands: Tall candle holders (usually made of wrought iron) stand on the floor to light a room. For an example, think of the floor-standing candelabras at weddings or the single stands you see in historic homes. Candle stands don't top the list for popularity as they did once.

Luminaria (paper bags of sand with votive candles inside), lawn and yard torches copied from ocean islands, and reproductions of ancient hanging lanterns are specialty candle-lighting devices that are all the rage at the moment. For the latest in candle-lighting paraphernalia, check out your mail-order catalogs.

A FEW CAUTIONARY NOTES

The enjoyment of candles in your home comes with a note or two of caution:

- Avoid wax spills by placing a dish, coaster, or bowl under every candle.

- Don't put candles directly on furniture. The oils from the candle could stain the surface.

- When you've lit a room with candlelight, make sure someone is in the room at all times.

- Use a candle snuffer to extinguish candle flames. It'll keep the wax from splattering and the wicks centered.

- Trim long wicks to a quarter inch for burning without smoke. A long wick burns faster and hotter.

- Allow wax drips to harden before removing them. You can melt them with a hair dryer and wipe them away with paper towels or freeze them and peel them off.

If you remember to respect fire, it will return the favor.

A COMPLETE WASTE OF TIME

The 3 Second-Worst Things to Do with Candles:

1. Buy candles too narrow for their holders.

2. Try to remove wax spills while they're still warm.

3. Burn them in the wind.

OCCASIONS YOU CAN HOLD A CANDLE TO

Lazy style comes to candle arranging with simple and elegant ideas for putting a magical spin on a special occasion. The following projects read like recipes and are probably easier to assemble than any cooking you've done.

Picnic Candle Pots

Pack a pair of candle pots to put in your next picnic pack. You'll be glad you did because the flames will highlight the evening hours as they drop away into the sunset.

You'll need

Two or three terra cotta pots

Plastic wrap

Sand

A dozen *thin* and tall tapers

Long-nosed lighter

1 Put a lining of plastic wrap at the bottoms of the pots (to keep sand from flowing out).

2 Fill the pots with sand.

3 Cover and wrap the pots with plastic wrap for transport to the picnic. (Skip this step if you're picnicking at home.)

4 When the witching hour nears, stand the tapers in the pots at slight angles so their flames don't touch. (They'll look something like the candle pots lit for religious rites in India.)

5 Light the candles and enjoy their presence at your picnic.

QUICK ☻ *PAINLESS*

Pull double-duty use out of your gardening pots by using them for picnic-pot tapers. When the occasion is past, they can resume their original role.

Dinnertime Salt Bowls

Bowls of bulk salt with tea lights tucked in their centers are inexpensive, easy ways to make a candle-lighting splash that's practically risk-free. Salt is naturally fire-retardant so sinking a tea light into a bowl of salt is a safe thing to do. Also, because the candle is contained inside a bowl, there's no danger of wax spilling onto a surface. Put a line-up of salt bowls on your mantel for added firelight sparkle, or place one at each table setting at your next dinner. Just keep the bowls out of reach of evergreens or plant material that could ignite.

Everything you need comes from the kitchen or grocery store:

Bowls from your kitchen or china cupboard

Bulk salt (sea salt or pickling salt)

Tea lights with tin or plastic wraps

Matches or a long-nosed lighter

1 Fill the bowls with salt to within an inch of the bowl tops.

2 Press a tea light into the center of each bowl of salt until the tea light is even with the salt level.

3 Set the bowls in the arrangement you've chosen.

4 Light the candles when they'll be most appreciated.

Dine By the Light of a Pool

Float a boatload of candles in a sea of water. Okay, float 8 or 10 floating candles in a large bowl of water and light them. They'll move and float about like little boats.

You'll need

A large, low ceramic, glass, or porcelain bowl
Water
8 or 10 floating candles
Long-nosed lighter

1 Fill a large bowl with water.

2 Float the candles on the water.

3 Light the candles with a long-nosed lighter. (Matches take too long.)

Holiday Light Pyramid

Cylindrical containers can do for candles what they do for flowers: show off their architecture. This project reminds me of the old-fashioned pyramids of candles that you see in windows of homes during the holidays.

Except for one thing—the style. Cylinders are firmly contemporary in their attitude, and I like this new take on the old pyramid idea. Arrange five look-alike cylinders on a window sill for floating candles. Here's how to create the pyramid effect: When you pour in the water, put the most in the central cylinder. Take the water level a step down in the cylinders flanking each side of the one in the center. The water levels of *the outside cylinders should be a step lower than the middle ones.*

Here's what you need to make a floating candle pyramid:

Five cylinders

Five floating candles

Water

Long-nosed lighter

1 Pour the water in the cylinders as described in the preceding paragraph.

2 Float the five floating candles on the water.

3 Light the candles.

Light a Dark Corner in an Instant

Large pillar candles are appealing more for their architecture than for the light they produce. Their stately columns have far greater impact than their tiny flames. Even so, you can light up a dark corner in an instant with a single pillar set on a plant stand. During daylight, you'll be left with a handsome candle that stands on its own without a light.

To make a candle stand, you'll need

Plant stand

Large pillar candle

Large bowl or tray (to fit under the candle)

Lemon or bay leaves (to spread around the candle inside the candle base)

Lighter

Tea light or votive candle

IF YOU'RE SO
INCLINED

Tuck greens in around the cylinders you've set in the windowsill. Because the candles are completely protected, there's no danger of fire.

1 Set the plant stand in its place.

2 Set the tray (or bowl) on the stand.

3 Set the pillar on the tray.

4 Circle the pillar with lemon or bay leaves.

5 Light the candle for a special occasion.

6 When (and if) the pillar candle shows signs of not wanting to stay lit for long, set the tea light or votive in the hollow at the center of the pillar. Light that instead of trying to keep the pillar lit.

Light-a-Ledge for Legendary Nights

Line up a long series of votive candles on an open ledge to create a stunning, room-changing effect. Just be sure you don't choose a ledge that's under another ledge (a shelf under another shelf). If you do, you'll singe the shelf above it and eventually start a fire.

For this lighting effect, you need open shelving, such as a fireplace mantel, a sideboard, the top of a sideboard, or window sills. This is an especially effective candlelight treat in a contemporary home with architectural built-in window ledges around the upper parts of a room. If you choose a window ledge or sill for candles, be sure there are no curtains or draperies nearby.

You'll need

Votive candles in glass containers
Long-nosed lighter

1 Arrange the votive candles in a line on a ledge, making sure there's no danger of curtains, plant material, or over-ledges in the way of the flames.

2 Light the candles.

3 Take time to enjoy the effect with your friends.

Candles in the Wind

Twin pillars in twin urns (you'll need to match the diameters of the pillars to the diameters of the urn tops) are twice as nice as one. They'll look great as twin sconces on a mantel or as bookends on a long ledge of oversized books.

You'll need

Two urn-shaped flowerpots
Two pillar candles with the correct diameter for fitting into the urns
Lighter

1 Fit the pillars into the urns.

2 Stand the urns in a place on a mantel or a book ledge.

3 Light the candles for special occasions or leave them unlit to enjoy the architecture of the pillars.

YOU'LL THANK YOURSELF LATER

For inexpensive votive holders that look good together, buy a couple sets of six short drinking glasses. Choose the ones with frosted or beveled surfaces.

In the Mirror

You'll have twice the light if you place candles in front of a mirror. Try a few candles in an entry hall on a table in front of a hall mirror, or arrange several on a mantel with a mirror.

You'll need

Various candlesticks of the same material

Tapers to fit the candlesticks

Candle rings to catch wax drips

Mirror to reflect the light

Lighter

1 Fit the candles into the candlesticks by melting their bottoms and inserting them into the holders while the wax is still fluid. Straighten and steady the candles and allow a little time for the wax to firm up in the candlesticks.

2 Slip the candle rings over the candles to ensure that wax won't spill onto the surface below.

3 Arrange the candles on the mantel or table in front of the mirror.

4 Light the candles as needed.

IF YOU'RE SO
INCLINED

Buy decorative bobeches (candle rings) for your tapers to dress them up. Import stores and candle shops can show you basic wax-catching candle rings and decorative bobeches with hanging beads and baubles.

Dining Table Charms

The traditional dinner table candle arrangement is two tapered candles in twin candleholders. My grandmothers did it all the time. I give them top grades for smarts when it comes to timesaving, lazy devices. It takes no time at all to light a couple of candles that sit out on the table all day, every day.

For this dinner table arrangement—one with a group of candlesticks—spring for a little more style and don't worry about exactly how much time you're spending on it—that is, if you've fallen under the wily charms of the candle. If not, stick to the two-taper caper.

To go all out, you'll need

Five to seven candlesticks (of the same material)
White tapered candles to fit inside the candlesticks
Lighter

1 Fit the candles into the candlesticks by lighting their bottoms with the lighter to melt the wax.

2 Settle the candles into the hollows in the candlesticks, supporting and straightening them until the wax firms up and they can stand by themselves.

3 Light the candles for dinner.

QUICK ⚫ PAINLESS

Time-Traveler Chandelier

Take a trip back in time and shop for an old Victorian candelabra or floor-standing candle stand with several tiers or candle holders. Even a candle stand rented from a wedding supply store could be a wonderful addition to a room for a while.

You'll need

Candelabra (available in antiques shops, flea markets, and wedding rental stores)

Brass or silver cleaner

Rags

White tapers to fit the candleholders

Lighter

1 When you get your candelabra home, clean it with the appropriate cleaner if it's silver or brass. Follow the instructions on the cleaner's label. If it's a painted or wooden candelabra, give it a good wipe-down.

2 Fit the tapers into the holders by melting the bottoms with the lighter. Insert them into the holders. Straighten and support them until the wax firms up and they can stand alone.

3 Light the candles for an occasion. When the occasion is over, they'll still be beautiful just standing in their places in the room.

Getting Time on Your Side

	The Old Way	The Lazy Way
Cleaning up a wax spill	30 minutes	10 minutes
Deciding on what candles go together	An hour	A minute or two
Mixing and matching a group of candlesticks	30 minutes	10 minutes
Fitting a candle to a holder	2 trips to the candle store	1 trip: You took the holder with you
Cleaning wax out of holders	Scraping and smearing	Heating or freezing, then removing
Arranging candles	20 minutes	5 minutes

Last-Minute Styling Tricks

Show me the money—the easy way out of getting up to speed for company. Where is it written that cleaning house and super-hosting should head the list of things you want to do when you grow up? I'd rather be lying facedown on my pillow in bed, on a warm beach, or on the massage table getting the stress knots smoothed out of my back.

It's not easy being clean—or ready for company at any moment. The upkeep is too much when you've got a million other things on your plate. For most of the day, the house is a littered mess of scattered toys and laundry and the ordinary, cluttered jetsam of people living their lives. You really wouldn't want to expose it to television cameras or the world at large. You'd like at least five minutes' notice before someone stops by—better yet, a date noted on a calendar. That would be a luxury: You'd know just how much time you had before they came knocking on your door. What you'd like most of all is a list of the laziest ways to get your company act together.

SHORT STOPS

Back-door friends can stop by any time. Whether you're cleaned-up or messy, they love you and your home just the way you are. Front-door friends are the ones that put you on edge. Here's the quickest formula for getting rooms company-ready. (I'm assuming things are generally picked up, if not thoroughly cleaned.)

The Five Minute Run-Through

Take a minute for each one of these "fluffing-up" moves before your guests knock on the door. It'll take five one-minute fixes:

- Plump up the pillows on the sofas and chairs where you and your guests will sit. Just be sure you haven't piled on too many pillows and left no room for sitting.

- Run a lamb's wool duster over noticeably dusty surfaces. A lamb's wool duster is better than a feather duster because it doesn't shed wool the way feather dusters' feathers fly.

- Straighten the pictures on the wall. You don't have to get out the level; just give it your best eye.

- Hit the lights to set the right mood, especially in the entry. A warm, inviting lamp glow upon entering tells your guests you've prepared the way for them.

- Last, but not least, spill some fruit into a bowl so you'll have something appetizing to look at in the room. Always beautiful and perfect, fruit and flowers give a room vitality.

Your guests will notice your decorating efforts and repay you with their best manners. You won't admit that it took you only five measly minutes.

Bathroom Break

Inevitably, someone asks to use the bathroom. The hair on the back of your neck stands on end if you haven't done a quick once-over before they came.

Take five:

- Do a quick pick-up, removing dirty towels and scattered bathroom toys.

- Check the mirror for spatters and splatters. Give it the window-cleaner slap if it's not shining bright.

- Light a votive candle that's in a safe container so they can find the light switch. Besides, everything looks better in candlelight.

- Supply a dispenser of anti-bacterial liquid soap so they don't have to use family soap bars.

- Hang up clean, non-intimidating towels so that when they wash their hands they won't be afraid to use them.

It's the *least* you can do.

A FEW GOOD REASONS

No doubt, you're a generous person and won't quibble over extra work when it comes to celebrations. After all, these are the days of your life (sounds like a soap opera), and they won't come again. You'll think of your own reasons for celebrating. Here are a few of mine:

IF YOU'RE SO
INCLINED

Got a couple extra minutes? Light a candle on the coffee table for the good scents of burning wax and fire. Pick a bloom from your window garden and float it in a bowl of water near the candle.

- The afternoon chat room, bridge game, or lunch with the smaller powers-that-be could use a wake-up call in the redecorating department.

- It'll be in living color—the game, that is. Well, so will the munchies and the dishes they're in.

- The beggars are coming. It's banquet time for your relatives. Whether it's for the holidays, a post-wedding breakfast, or an annual reunion, it's your turn to do the innovating that will transform the family occasion into something they'll care to remember.

- It's black-tie night at your house. You had a temporary lapse of common sense (think of the time it could take) and invited six guests for dinner. Get out the big guns.

- They're coming for an overnight. They'll notice your bedside manners, bathrooms, and food service.

When you commit to a celebration, be sure you can afford the time to do it. If not, think about hiring a caterer or soliciting help from someone who has the time.

FOOD SERVICE WITH A STYLE: YOU'RE IN GOOD COMPANY

My favorite "let's-eat-out" spot is a sleek, contemporary diner that serves terrific food in a clean and simple no-nonsense restaurant style. It's no-frills eating at its best. That doesn't mean it's not a visually appealing experience. I love the shiny, stainless-steel countertops, everyday salts and peppers, gleaming chrome pots, and snappy, black-and-white menus. Takes me back to a time

when real diners were a hot and serious trend. Only this time around (the second time around is always better), it's a lot more fun because this diner sees itself in the history mirror and doesn't take itself quite so seriously. I call it tongue-in-chic design and take it right on home with me.

Diner style is based on the classic premise that plain, white dishes are first-rate when it comes to framing food to its finest advantage. Unlike dishes with loud, disruptive designs, they stay quietly in the background, out of the competition for best of show.

You can pick a lazy diner style to suit any occasion. It's easy to translate basic white dishes in a variety of ways to set the tone for a party and your good company. On the following pages, I show you how last-minute styling tricks can add up to big entertaining dividends.

Pure, Unadulterated Lazy-Way Dining

Classic white diner dishes are the mark of the uncomplicated nature of lazy-style dining. Add plain-and-shiny stainless steel flatware (requires no polishing), quality white-paper napkins, clear-glass drinking glasses, and you're set in five minutes.

Everyday style's a beautiful thing. It's graced by purity: Wooden toothpicks and grocery-store salt-and-pepper shakers that show you what's in them, a clear-glass pitcher of ice water clinking and sloshing inside when you pour it, and a fresh centerpiece of green salad in a great white bowl. You serve up helpings onto plates instead of dirtying serving bowls, and ask your diners to please pass the salad and dressings.

IF YOU'RE SO
INCLINED

Take advantage of housewares outlets to stock up on the basics for diner dishes. Crate and Barrel outlets carry some of the best at low prices. Also, check out discount stores and import stores, such as Pier 1 Imports.

To set a table diner style, you need

   White porcelain or ironstone plates and bowls

   Stainless-steel flatware and mixing bowls

   Large, white paper dinner napkins

   Clear glass tumblers

   Condiments in small white containers on a large white
      plate or tray

1 On a hard, impenetrable counter or table surface that are easy to wipe up, set the plates. (Reserve white tablecloths for special occasions.)

2 Lay each set of flatware across the dinner napkin diagonally and roll the napkin around the flatware.

3 Put the flatware on the left side of the plate.

4 Set the drinking tumblers to the upper right of the plate.

5 Pour ice water into the glasses from a clear glass pitcher.

6 Set the condiment tray within easy reach.

   Those are the basics. If you want to have more than everyday fun, add a little effort and transform your solid-citizen food service into something a little less expected.

YOU'LL THANK YOURSELF LATER

Have a plan for general clean-up so that it's easy and productive to do a last-minute run-through of the house before company arrives.

Black-Tie Affair

Just kidding about the black tie—but not about the dress-up style it suggests. Here's tongue-in-chic diner style at its best—a poor man's bread-and-soup supper with an attitude. A common, humble meal that's as dignified and elegant as any meal served in an uptown restaurant. It has split-screen personality: simple yet grand. It's all in how you style it.

You'll need

Eight snowy-white chargers (that's not horses; chargers are large, shallow plate-like dishes that collect liquid under plates or soup bowls)

Eight wide, white soup bowls

Eight sets of shiny-clean, stainless-steel butter knives and soup spoons

Eight water glasses

Eight wine glasses (optional)

Eight large, white cloth dinner napkins

A white tablecloth, preferably with a nub or texture that will contrast with the smooth, shiny surfaces of your dishes. You could use a new woven bedspread if the color and texture are beautiful.

Salt and freshly ground pepper served in eight personal salt-and-pepper sets or on small butter-pat dishes at each setting.

Two or three large white soup tureens with lids

White cheese platter

Butter bowl

IF YOU'RE SO INCLINED

When purchasing dinerware, it's okay to mix Chinese, French, and American porcelains as long as they have two things in common: Simple shapes and white color.

1 Set the table in a not-so-everyday place. I don't have a dining room so I set up a long, portable, and collapsible table in my living room by the fire.

2 Cover the table with the cloth.

3 Set the chargers.

4 Place the soup bowls on the chargers, the plain-folded napkins to the left of the chargers, and the flatware on the right.

5 Place the water glasses to the right above the flatware.

6 Place a single-serve loaf of bread on each napkin.

7 Fill the platter with cheese slices and the bowl with butter.

8 Fill the soup tureens with two or three hearty soups.

9 Invite your guests to the table.

You may have already served wine to your guests as an appetizer. Ask them to bring their glasses to the table where you can continue to serve them.

YOU'LL THANK YOURSELF LATER

Take the last-minute out of your preparations by working ahead on as many of the entertaining tasks as possible.

Blue Bottle Cafe

Relaxed dining is never easier than when you serve it bistro style. "Bistro" is a French word for a small, unpretentious tavern or cafe. Typically, it's associated with simplicity and freshness—blue-and-white dishes, checks and stripes, generous pitchers, plain flatware, bread and cheese, and wildflowers.

You can have the cafe look in half an hour if you have the right things on hand.

You'll need

Small, round tables with enough chairs to seat your guests

Everyday diner dishes and flatware

Blue-and-white checked and striped linens

Cobalt-blue spring-water (empty) bottles from the grocery store

Paper-lace doilies

Glass pitchers

Fresh, white daisies

It'll take just five five-minute styling tricks to pull it together. That's 25 minutes.

1 Place your tables so that seating is comfortable and accessible for everyone. You can arrange tables in front of loveseats and sofas or out in the room with two or more chairs. Allow about three feet between the backs of the closest chairs for ease in getting up and down.

2 Cover the tables with basic blue and white (or plain white) tablecloths and, if desired, layer a blue-and-white napkin over the tablecloth for addition pattern and texture.

IF YOU'RE SO
INCLINED

Serve spring water in the same style as the blue bottles you've emptied for vases. It'll double the impact of the brilliant, cobalt-blue color.

3 Set the tables with white dishes and water glasses. Lay a blue-and-white checked or striped napkin on the plate and lay the flatware on the napkin.

4 Fill the blue bottles with water and slip a stem or three of daisies into the water for each table's bouquet. If you're all dining at the same table, fill a salad bowl with potted daisies for the center of the table.

5 Add a clear pitcher of ice water, salts and peppers, oils and vinegars, and breads and cheeses on breadboards (lined with paper lace), and you're ready. If you have a lemon, slice it thinly and slip it into the ice water.

Family Banquet on a Shoestring

The furniture and tabletop accessories you find in rental stores aren't just for weddings. They also fit home banquets that celebrate family occasions. For a little money and less effort (so many relatives, so many helping hands), you'll breeze through the bigger diner-style dinners of your life with a lot of energy, enthusiasm, and innovative ideas.

You'll need

Eight-foot rented "church" tables

White folding chairs (rented)

Freestanding candelabra with white candles (rented and optional)

White paper table coverings from the party store or white linen fabric yardage or clean sheets to fit the tables

Small white pitchers and large mugs

White dinner plates, bowls, cups, and saucers (yours plus additional dishes borrowed from *The Lazy Way* friends)

Clear drinking glasses or stemware

Stainless-steel flatware (yours plus borrowed)

Several sets of see-through salts and peppers

Clear-glass water pitchers

Tabletop "reserved" signs from the party store

One type of flowers purchased in bulk (mixing flowers cuts down on your purist style)

Place cards

1 Move the rented furniture into the dining areas.

2 Cover the tables with cloths.

3 Set the tables in diner style as described in the earlier part of this chapter.

4 Put reserved signs on the table.

5 Ask someone to make and set out place cards.

6 Plan the buffet food service. You might need to make separate areas: a main course buffet, a drinks counter, and a dessert buffet.

7 Ask someone to arrange the flowers in the white pitchers and mugs and put them on the tables.

8 Ask someone to arrange the dessert buffet.

When you're ready to serve the food, tell everyone to find their places, pick up their plates, and help themselves at the various buffets. After they're seated, don't ask them to get up for the rest of the meal. (Seating will probably be tight.) Ask

QUICK ⬛ PAINLESS

You can save money on rented furniture if you pick up and return it yourself. You might need to ask a friend with a van to help you.

someone to pour the ice water and keep the drinks supplied. For seconds, pass the buffet food platters around.

Give everyone a break until dessert time so you and your many-handed elves have a chance to do a major clean-up. When the time seems right, call your guests to the dessert bar.

Catching the Big Game

They're coming over for the Orange Bowl, the Rose Bowl, or the Sugar Bowl. Who could keep track of it all? Break out the diner-style plastics (they'll be too busy to notice how you're sneaking out of work), and supply them with a self-serve buffet of all the couch-potato treats you can think of. Then, sit back and enjoy the day with them.

You'll need

Paper party set-ups (colorful napkins, plates, flatware, and hot-and-cold cups)

Big, passable silver-metallic plastic platters and bowls (available in party stores)

Galvanized buckets of ice to cool drinks

Extra seating, pillows, and blanket wraps

1 Assemble the extra seating, pillows, and wraps.

2 Assemble the serving platters and bowls.

3 Ice down the drinks.

4 Call in the troops.

Dining Alfresco

Take it outside where the eating's fine. Why does everything taste better outdoors? Whether it's a porch party, a barbecue on the patio, or a potluck on the beach, outdoor dining can't be matched for unabashedly off-the-cuff food service. It takes only one strategy when it comes to style: Keep it simple and bright.

Fold-up furniture is useful but takes work to transport and assemble. You could take your tabletop cues from traditional picnickers and sit on the grass or sand. For a portable party that goes on into the evening, you'll need

Portable furniture (optional)

Portable grill (optional)

Ice chests filled with ice

Galvanized buckets and bushels for icing down drinks

Empty tin-can tumblers for wildflowers

Wicker hampers to fill with food and the rest of the items on this list

Sturdy, white paper plates and napkins

Clear-glass jelly jars or plastic tumblers

Food nets

Red-and-white plaid, checked, or striped dishtowels for tabletop spreads, food wraps, place mats, or napkins (if you don't want to use paper)

Paper towels

Red or white paper tablecloths

Empty jelly jars with votive candles

Matches

Blankets

Bug spray
Citronella torches (optional)
Wildflowers

1 Transport everything to the site.

2 Hunt for stones to weight fly-away papers.

3 Transfer ice from the chest to galvanized buckets and ice down the drinks. Set the buckets to the side for self-service.

4 Cover a table or two with paper cloths or spread blankets on the ground.

5 Transfer the food and food service onto the tabletops.

6 Fill tin cans with water and weight them with stones before adding wildflowers.

From here on, anything can happen. With a potluck, the element of surprise will add to the fun. This is your chance for impromptu dining.

BED AND BREAKFAST

Overnight guests require special attention, even if you're just meeting their basic needs for a comfortable bed and a hot breakfast. Your room at the inn will be like a stay at a good hotel.

YOU'LL THANK YOURSELF LATER

Call ahead to make sure your picnic destination will be open when you arrive. Nothing is more disappointing than a closed-out party.

It'll take five five-minute styling tricks:

- Make up the beds with fresh sheets and lay an extra blanket or comforter across the foot of each bed.

- If there isn't a phone to plug in, leave a cellular phone in a basket with pens and notepads on the bedside table. Supply telephone numbers you think your guest could use.

- Lay a stack of picture books on the bedside table, and set a candle in a holder on the book stack. Supply a book of matches to light the candle.

- Arrange a vase of flowers for the bedside table and set it next to a water carafe.

- Supply hotel-white towels, a bathrobe, and bath luxuries to suit your guests.

That's the *least* you can do. If you're inclined toward generosity, take your cues from pleasant hotel stays you've had and try to repeat their services at home. It might mean room service (breakfast in bed) or advice on sights in your area that your guests many enjoy.

YOU'LL THANK YOURSELF LATER

Keep guest-room supplies separate from everyday family stuff to keep its hotel-white freshness.

Getting Time on Your Side

	The Old Way	The Lazy Way
Setting an everyday table	10 minutes	5 minutes
Pulling off a family banquet	48 hours	24 hours
Assembling a casual party	4 hours	2 hours
Preparing an impromptu picnic	6 hours	2 hours
Getting your company act together	10 minutes	5 minutes
Providing for an overnight stay	2 hours	1 hour

Chapter seventeen

Stretching Out Your Living Space

Lazy is as lazy does. In a rush of enthusiasm, *The Lazy Way* pushes back the constraints of work, pulls out the casual decorating stops, and opens up the dance floor so the good-living times can roll. This chapter is about the ephemeral, outdoor sides of your home and all the temporary play spaces you can create to expand your horizons.

You were probably a kid once. Except for hard-driving, self-promoting, get-ahead super-humans, most people were. We fantasized about and acted upon our desires for dwellings somewhere outside the boundaries of home—such as tree houses, sand castles, and snow forts.

You don't have to be a kid to qualify for additional real estate. If you're in a technical grown-up world hemmed in by tight work spaces, heavy schedules, and little contact with sunlight, plant life, or cool, calm water, you're deprived.

Come up for air. Come *out* for air. You can stake a claim under the trees or sky, near the water, on a ledge, or in a protected spot to sit back and absorb the natural sensations of wind, water, earth, and sky.

YOU DESERVE A BREAK

Make plans to revive your sense of well-being. Take redecorating outside where the assembly is lazy. Decorating out-of-doors is pretty much the same as decorating inside, except that its easier. More casual. Carefree. Careless, even.

For starters, here's a list of simple getaways:

- Re-made in the shade: A shady getaway can be a folding chair and a cup of coffee on an urban patio, a suburban hammock hung between two trees, or a rural retreat under a lilac bush. It's created on the spot for magic moments: a private place for reading a newspaper on Sunday morning or a stop at the end of the day to contemplate a crisp, October night by pumpkin light.

- Kitchen garden: Whether it's a picketed window box on a counter, a window ledge where you grow herbs for cooking, or a vegetable plot outside your back door, the kitchen garden becomes part of your home-again landscape.

- Arbor day: Sit under a garden trellis and tell your secrets; whisper your wishes under a palm tree. Find shelter under an old oak tree or a structure that acts like one.

- Terrace hill: Catch the scenery from an urban rooftop, a suburban sun deck, or a rural bank high

A COMPLETE WASTE OF TIME

The 3 Worst Things to Do While Making a Private Getaway:

1. Tell someone you're doing it.

2. Keep your cell phone turned on.

3. Leave on an empty gas tank.

above a rolling river. Whatever the view, it's sure to revive your soul.

- Garden plot: Owned or leased, in your backyard or miles away, the garden plot puts you in touch with the earthy frontier along the outer edge of your life.

- Courtyard protection: The walls of a courtyard keep free spirits safe from wind and predators.

- Lean-to style: Beach-hut tents, garden sheds, awnings, and cabanas assembled from fabric and cobbled-together boards give you that on-vacation feeling without you getting on a plane or sweating it out too long with the kids in the car.

- Greenhouse: Make your greenhouse as humble as pots in a window bursting with color, as bold as a crowded bay window garden, or as full-blown as an added-on, glassed-in greenhouse with a terra cotta floor.

- Porches where you want to be: If you're lucky enough to have one of these attached to your house, your closest getaway is just outside the door.

- Blanket in the park: The edges of a blanket mark the perimeter of a sparkling Fourth of July under the fireworks or a childish romp under a tree. It can give you a comfortable lookout from a mountaintop or a vineyard hill.

Fold away the technology. (Okay, take the cell phone.) Pack up a getaway and move it on out. Keep it as simple as possible so it doesn't feel like work.

Make secret plans for being lazy. Then, carry them out.

The Lazy Way

TAKING IT OUTSIDE

Outdoor furniture doesn't stay in one place for long, especially if it's not weather-proof and it was borrowed from indoors for an off-the-cuff occasion. When weather becomes inclement or wintered over, even the most weather-worthy furniture needs shelter.

You can place outdoor furniture in three groups:

- Chairs
- Tables
- Beds

If you want to and have good reason, you could spend a good piece of change on weather-hardy, three-season outdoor furniture—the kind that stays permanently in place on a well-seasoned porch, deck, or terrace. Such setups include barbecue grills and serious coolers and bars under umbrellas. To purchase those, you can find seasonal, casual furniture stores in your area. They'll supply you with suggestions and ways to use their products.

This chapter goes *The Lazy Way*. That means no big furniture commitments, setups, or changes—just the simplest means for assembling quickly improvised outdoor occasions. The following list includes inexpensive, transportable, collapsible, fold-up stuff with a go-anywhere, do-anything attitude.

Chairs and Sofas to Sit on

Casual outdoor seating is available everywhere. For the most inexpensive seating, pull out the fold-up pieces you have in your house or apartment—the kind you bought

YOU'LL THANK YOURSELF LATER

Don't commit to big outdoor furniture purchases unless you're sure you're ready to settle in and stay at home for leisure time activities. For now, create some simple retreats you can try one at a time.

when you first set up home. If you like the look of plastic, you can buy inexpensive pre-formed, stackable chairs for a porch, patio, or deck. These chairs don't travel well, however, so check the list for three fold-up ideas. The list also includes getaway furniture that's built into the landscape:

- Folding directors chairs
- Folding chairs made from wood, metal, plastic, and aluminum
- Wooden fold-up lawn and deck chairs with canvas sling seats
- Slatted, fold-up deck chairs
- Aluminum lawn chairs
- Wooden stools and chairs
- Wicker sofas and rockers
- Built-in benches
- Wooden or cast-iron park benches
- Junk-store dining chairs

Antiques shops, garage sales, and flea markets are the best place to find funky, inexpensive, and full-of-character outdoor furniture. Home stores and mail-order catalogs can sell you the new stuff that's more collapsible and transportable than what's sold at serious patio furniture stores.

QUICK ⬤ PAINLESS

Invest in casual, washable, canvas fabrics for pillows, tablecloths, and cushions or seating for your outdoor chairs.

IF YOU'RE SO
INCLINED

Buy a pre-cut, RTA (ready-to-assemble) picnic table and bench kit from the home center or lumberyard. Choose one with benches that are assembled separately from the table so you can move the set around your yard with ease.

Tables to Dine on

You can't dance on the tops of these tables. They might collapse!

- Picnic tables and benches
- Lightweight fold-up picnic tables
- Round, metal cafe tables
- Wooden garden tables
- Folding side tables
- TV trays
- Potting benches

Buy these pieces in the same places you buy your chairs. You'll have fun creating your own personal style of casual dining.

Beds to Sleep on

Gather furniture to stretch out on so you can imagine yourself sunning on a cruise ship deck, swinging in a Caribbean hammock, or drifting in a river canoe:

- Fold-up camp cots
- Aluminum-framed lounges
- Wooden steamer chairs
- Hammocks

Camping stores carry hammocks and camp cots and a lot of collapsible furniture you can fold up and carry with you. Buy some mosquito netting while you're there. Oh, and they have good portable grills and lanterns, too.

Accessorize the Outdoors

Contemporary life is in love with home accessories. Last Christmas, clothing stores suffered poor sales, but home accessories flew out the door. Times are good for building a nest and finding things to feather it:

- Soft stuff: Apply *The Lazy Way* of choosing indoor fabrics to the out-of-doors as well. Keep it natural so your redecorating will stay in touch with the elements. Color-wise, choose canvas whites (to reflect the light and expand the spaces visually), cool, soft Caribbean blues of sky and sea, and lightweight greens of grass and leaves. When it comes to patterns, keep them simple. Stay with stripes, checks, and open, loose plaids. Apply them to chair covers, pillows, canvas awnings, blankets, napkins, and table coverings. Plan to remove most of the fabrics when the retreat is over unless you've covered a table with an attractive plastic tablecloth that can stand a wash of rain.

- Containers: This part of the decorating is the easiest because it's catch-as-catch-can. Let the containers cross your path on their own. You'll recognize their worth when you see them coming—rain barrels, old sinks, tubs, terra cotta pots, tin cans, galvanized metal buckets, tabletop trays, and myriad other things you'll spot at flea markets, discount stores, home stores, and antiques shops, not to mention mail-order catalogs.

YOU'LL THANK YOURSELF LATER

Keep a supply of bug spray and sunscreen on hand in anticipation of a series of outings.

■ Lighting: Supply yourself with your heart's desire of lanterns, candles, or strings of electric lights.

Your casual accessory inventory will build up quickly. It's the most carefree decorating you'll ever do.

MAKING A GETAWAY AT HOME

My first getaway was a tree house, a humble affair consisting of a three-plank-wide platform balanced in the gracious crook of a maple tree. Three board steps, nailed to the trunk of the tree, allowed easy access to my narrow nest.

Anyone was welcome there. The only password was a need for refuge or recreation. This was high ground, a sacred bower free from the grown-up world below. You could go there to read in the company of squirrels and listen to birds converse. You could explore private feelings and know your independent thoughts. You could hear the songs in your heart.

Happiness Is a Hammock

Now, my tree house is a hammock hung over a ridge between an apple tree and a "volunteer" tree of doubtful origin. It doesn't matter to me that the volunteer is considered "junk" by horticulturists; its sturdy trunk is just the right distance from the apple tree to conveniently support my portable retreat. Leaves shingle my roof overhead and squirrels scurry about. Sometimes, friends come to sit in the weathered cedar chairs my husband built for my outdoor room.

A COMPLETE WASTE OF TIME

The 3 Worst Things to Do with Your Outdoor Stuff:

1. Never take time to use it.

2. Leave it out all winter.

3. Loan it out and not get it back.

I've made peace with the freeway that runs past our house three doors down. Instead of hearing the rhythms of passing cars and trucks, I translate the movement as wind gusts blowing through an imaginary forest.

Farmhouse Porch

An attached porch has all the elements of a room inside the house, except, perhaps, for permanent, weather-worthy walls. All the comforts of home are just inside the door. This is your chance to simplify all those indoor comforts and take out to the porch only the bare necessities. Make it a vacation without all the baggage.

Fortunately, once you've moved the furniture out for the season, it'll be ready for any occasion. All you'll need is a little food, drink, and a reason to celebrate.

To set up your porch, you'll need

Wicker sofa or porch swing

Junk-store tables and chairs

Wooden benches

Plants

Rag rugs

Tool box for napkins, dishtowels, and flatware

Galvanized metal containers

Quilts (optional)

1 If you're lucky enough to have a porch swing, your main piece of furniture is already in place. If not, place the wicker sofa at the end of the porch or against a wall where it can be the center of attraction or the anchor in the furniture arrangement.

2 Place the main table in front of the wicker sofa or as a buffet table at the opposite end of the porch.

3 Set the chairs, benches, and small tables in casual spots so they can be easily moved and rearranged for different groups of people.

4 Spread the rugs on the floor.

5 Add plants in corners to soften the edges of the room.

6 Bring out the toolbox and metal containers full of food for food service when an occasion comes up.

7 Soften the seating with quilts.

ANYWHERE GETAWAYS

Improvise a different situation each time you make a personal getaway. For example, take a chair and a sandwich out for lunch under a pine tree in your backyard. Or get up in the dark, grab a fast-food coffee and bagel on the way, and sit on the beach for a sunrise watch.

Quick getaways are designed to take you back in time and out of the way of the speeding train of phones, faxes, pagers, and computers. Destinations? Spaces that encourage you to languish over a book, smell a scented rosebush, explore a patch of wild grass, and catch a trail of bird tracks over wet sand.

For ultimately simple retreats, you need

- A fold-up chair (optional)

- A book (optional)

- Something to eat or drink (optional)

- Yourself (not optional)

I leave the instructions up to you. You'll design the retreat to suit your needs and the time of year. Vary it. Invent. Just be sure you carry out your plans.

YOU'LL THANK YOURSELF LATER

Keep a thermos in your car for hot or cold drinks on your way to an escape. You'll have the vacation feeling by the time you arrive.

Arbor Dwelling

A vine-covered terrace dining room with built-in benches is the ideal and permanent setup for an arbor dwelling. A large, rectangular table runs down the center of the space, and the benches built inside the walls of the arbor serve as seating along the long sides of the table.

When you don't have the ideal arrangement in your backyard, an arbor or trellis you can move into, you can create a reasonable substitute with a tree in your backyard or in a public park. Here's how.

You'll need

A broad, expansive tree
Picnic table and benches
Table covering
Pillows (optional)
Lanterns
Ribbons

1 Stake your claim under a tree.

2 Have someone help you move in the picnic table and benches.

3 Cover the table with the covering.

4 Hang the lanterns from the tree branches or set them on the table.

5 For a festive occasion, tie ribbons from the tree branches to mark the site and watch the wind blow them around.

6 Light the lanterns in the evening hours.

Sand Castle

Get grounded in an ocean of sand and washed up with water. If you must, take your laptop, but I don't recommend it.

Homesteading on the sand comes as naturally as the rising and setting of the sun and hardly needs instruction. You can pick it up by watching what other beach bums do. Some arrangements are elaborate, some simple. It all depends on how many people are involved in the claim and how much energy they have for assembling it.

For a keep-it-simple setup, you'll need

Beach umbrella(s)

Large beach towels

Folding chairs

Cooler with iced drinks

Picnic basket with food

Sunscreen

1 Stake a claim on the beach.

2 Position the umbrella to shield you from the sun.

3 Spread the towels.

4 Set the chairs.

5 Dig in to the sand, the surf, the cooler, and the sunscreen.

YOU'LL THANK YOURSELF LATER

When you come home from a day at the beach, store the furniture and accessories in one place. The next time you want to go, you'll be ready in an instant.

URBAN STRETCHES

If city boundaries cut off your supplies of green grass, open air, and fresh water, and walks in the public park don't quite satisfy your appetite for sitting under your own private apple tree, create a garden right inside the walls of your apartment. It starts with as much open-air space as you can pull together.

Here are some things you can do to clear the decks:

- Downsize your possessions so you'll have more floor and wall space. Dark, heavy furniture takes up visual volume in a room, so, if you have a choice, choose light furniture with little ornamentation. Lazy furniture is naturally light and uncomplicated in pattern.

- Paint the walls in a light and airy color. Paint an accent wall in a pale green tone that speaks to you of the outdoors.

- Arrange seating groups or dining areas near the windows to be in the light as much as possible. If brick walls dominate the view, invest in ethereal window coverings that cut off the view but let in the light.

- Buy bedroom furniture that folds out for special uses and folds back up again. One of the oldest ideas is the Murphy bed that folds down from the wall for sleeping. Lofted beds give you floor spaces below the sleeping decks and, in effect, double your square footage. Trundle beds, bunk beds, and sofa beds are easy foldouts that quickly tuck away again.

QUICK ⬤ PAINLESS

To choose a garden accent wall color, go for the pale greens and blue-greens. Read color names that sound like what you're looking for—Jade Bath, Spruce Frost, Pale Apple, and Sea-Glass Green—and buy a quart to sample when you get home.

- Re-think your cooking and dining surfaces. A table with simple seating benches can fold up against a wall like a Murphy bed, and the benches get tucked underneath it and out of the way. You can have built-in dining sets with four chairs that collapse into a slim 10-inch-wide slot against a wall. Kitchen equipment can pull down from the ceiling for use.

- Compact your storage into highly organized spaces. For example, a twin bed can be built over two sets of dresser drawers and flanked at the ends by closets, all in a narrow space at the end of a room. An armoire can hold an entire entertainment center if you don't buy oversized electronic equipment.

- Mount your bicycle on a wall as a piece of functional art.

Now for the garden part.

YOU'LL THANK YOURSELF LATER

Make a wish list of furnishings you'd like to own or collections you'd like to create. Believe anything is possible and let yourself dream about what you really want.

Bamboo accessories can help you translate your indoor garden into a quiet place of Zen. Trays of sand, combed into patterns, give you a virtual reality of the perfect beach.

The Indoor Garden

You'll need

- Round cafe tables
- Garden furniture
- Patio pillows
- Water fountain or birdbath
- Small and large stones
- Green plants
- Trees
- Lanterns and candles
- Garden ornaments (old gate or pieces of iron gates, sculpted garden pieces)

1 Arrange the bistro tables in your seating group by the window for al fresco dining. You could place one directly in front of the window with two or three slim cafe chairs for sit-down dining. You could also use two small tables in place of a coffee table near cushioned seating pieces.

2 Fluff up the seating area with patio pillows.

3 Place the water fountain on an end table or settle it in a birdbath (no water) near a window.

4 Line it with smooth river stones and add a stone-sculpted bird when the perfect one turns up.

5 Stand trees where they'll best provide overhead shelter for you and get enough light and moisture for themselves.

6 Fill out the room with garden ornaments, plants, and stones.

City Edens

You've done what you could to bring the outside in, but you still long for some outdoor space that's yours. Do you have a windowsill or ledge? It's a start.

Living on the Ledge

This getaway is more a state of mind than a place to go. It's for cooped-up high-rise dwellers who need a sense of green in a city of concrete. Call it a virtual reality or a garden in the making.

To plot your ledge garden, consume the contents of tin-can food containers, wash them, and remove the labels. Tin cans are truly inexpensive to collect and have sleek, modern, environmentally friendly appeals. They're a welcome departure from terra cotta and flowerpots. When you have a good supply of tin cans of various sizes, start your garden.

You'll need

Empty tin cans

Small plants in small nursery pots

Potting soil

Medium-size nursery pot liners with drainage holes (pots to grow in)

Water

Scoop

Garden tray

QUICK ◖▦◗ PAINLESS

Shopping for your tin-can-chic containers? Get out your measuring tape and look for four-inch diameters. Forty-nine-ounce chicken broth cans are good, too.

1 When you get your plants home, water them in the kitchen sink and let them drain for a half hour.

2 Set them in tin cans with diameters that match. (The pots should rise just above the edges of the tin cans for easy removal when watering.)

3 Arrange the tin-can flowerpots in the garden tray (tin cans untreated by zinc will leave rusty rings on a surface) and set the tray on a window sill or a ledge under the window.

4 Water the plants as they require, removing them from the cans and letting them drain in the sink.

5 Return them to the can containers.

When plants outgrow their small pots, replant them in larger galvanized tin containers (galvanized tin is treated with zinc to prevent rust) or plant them in an outdoor garden.

Balcony Seats

A balcony works like a front porch—a permanent attachment to your home that's always handy for fresh-air breaks and watching the neighborhood go by. You'll avoid the hassle of moving indoor furniture outside every time you take a breather.

You'll need

Round metal cafe table
Plastic and metal folding chairs
Electric light strings
Extension cord
Votive candles

IF YOU'RE SO
INCLINED

Keep rainproof furniture on your balcony to encourage your outdoor habit.

1. String the lights on the balcony railing, wrapping them securely around the posts.

2. Attach the extension cord (you'll unplug it from the socket each time you go in for the night) to the light string and arrange for its attachment to the electric socket.

3. Arrange the table and chairs.

4. Light the candles for the evening. Bring them inside to keep them from the rain.

Rooftop Garden

When there's no place to go but up, urban pioneers hit the roof to take in the rain, the sun, the greens, and the earth. Much of it, especially the earth and greenery parts, has to come up through an elevator, but it can be done. It's no worse than carrying stone through the lower level of a townhouse to make a garden in a closed-in courtyard.

This rooftop setup gathers together the natural elements you've been deprived of in the workplace—earth, air, fire, and water. Rain caught in a barrel is the main source of drinking water for the plants. (You'll need to water often.) If you have no watering spigot close by, keep your garden plants to a minimum.

IF YOU'RE SO
INCLINED

Check local discount, party, and fabric stores for attractive blue-and-white or green-and-white plastic cloth-backed table coverings. You can leave them outside all summer.

To assemble a rooftop garden, you'll need

Rain barrel

Green plants in pots

Watering can

Trellises to line a wall (optional)

Garden tools in a metal container

Old metal chairs, bench, and table

Green-and-white plastic table covering

Software (pillows, blankets)

1 Find a rain barrel or water collecting containers first. It's key to your gardening setup. It could be a single, large container that could get murky over time or a series of galvanized metal (or serene white plastic) containers that are easily emptied and washed out so they can start collecting again.

2 Gather the garden pieces over time and take them out onto the roof. See this as a work in progress and keep its assembly like a tiny, quiet dream you're working on, even though you're working hard at your job. Today, you bring home a few plants from the corner stall. Tomorrow, it's a tin-can flowerpot you've emptied in the kitchen. Drag out the pleasures for as long as you can. It'll keep you going to the top for air.

3 Arrange the furniture as you gather it.

4 Keep a stash of fabrics you've reserved for the roof inside your apartment. Take them out whenever you need them.

YOU'LL THANK YOURSELF LATER

Imports stores are good sources for casual furnishings. They carry a lot of lightweight porch wicker as well as fold-up furniture, and the price is right.

Gardens of the Mind

When urban boundaries are so narrow that your home is little more than a sleeping nook and a place to hang your clothes, you have the power to expand your real estate in a sort of inward way. The world waits for you on the street, inviting you to feel its energetic pulses and step inside its public spaces to absorb their beauty and live there for a moment.

Nothing matches standing in the high-rising volumes of a cathedral lit by a thousand candles and scented by hot wax and fragrant incense. When you step out the side doors, you might discover a courtyard of apple trees in May bloom.

Nothing compares to standing in the atrium at Bendel's and taking in the scents of an extravagant Christmas tree hung with wicker baskets, each filled with a different type of whole herbs. Mentally step inside wonderful window displays and find a decorating idea you can tuck into your apartment.

No feeling comes close to the one you get when you choose a single, glorious bloom from a florist shop and take it home to your room where you let it take you back to the garden a hundred times before it fades. Very little is needed for a beautiful life; it's all within yourself and how you think about what you have.

Congratulations. You've learned how to enjoy the outdoors without having your own backyard. Walk until you're in need of rest. Enjoy the city's fountains, toss pennies in wishing wells, and skip stones on ponds. Take in the fragrances of greens and flowers, and absorb the sun when you find breaks in the shade.

The Lazy Way

Getting Time on Your Side

	The Old Way	The Lazy Way
Building a deck	Weeks of carpentry	Retreat to a plot of wild grass or newly mown grass under a tree
Setting up and cleaning a grill	Use a charcoal grill	Use a self-starting gas grill
Going on retreat	Heavy-duty plans	Lightweight plans
Setting up patio furniture	Buy expensive, seasonal furniture to assemble	Take indoor chairs outside
Assembling a picnic	Do it all yourself	Go potluck
Planting and tending a garden	10 hours a week	2 hours a week

More Lazy Stuff

How to Get Someone Else to Do It

Sooner or later, you'll want to hire a professional to help you with your redecorating. "Where do I start?" is your big question. My best answer: Word of mouth. Ask your friends, neighbors, and co-workers. They'll know the ins and outs of the professionals they've used. Reserve the Yellow Pages for times when you can't find someone to ask.

Sometimes, you can consult a local interior designer (expect to pay hourly fees) to get started on a number of projects. If you feel comfortable about it, you can have the designer handle the hiring out (again, you'll pay for the service) of smaller jobs for you. Here are some of the kinds of redecorating experts you might want to hire:

- Carpenters: Don't strain yourself trying to do carpentry you weren't born to do. Built-in cupboards and cabinetry jobs belong to the serious carpenter.

- Electricians: The law will keep you from doing built-in electrical work you aren't qualified for. You get the easy part: choosing a fixture and flicking the switch.

- Carpet and tile layers: Let the professionals cover your floors with carpet, tile, or wood. They'll know the rules of the game, and you can sit on the sidelines and supervise.

- Painters and paper hangers: A wall or two is within reason for you, but if you're not a dyed-in-the-wool do-it-yourselfer, hire a professional to give your woodwork and walls an overall refresher coat.

- Upholsterers: When your upholstery wears through, spring for a custom upholstery job.

- Furniture finishers: Simple refinishing is within your means, but who needs overwhelming fumes and mounds of sanding dust at home? Take complicated furniture makeovers out of the house.

- Drapers: Sometimes, a window makeover requires drapery sewing. You don't even own a sewing machine, let alone an iron to press up the fabric. Find someone who wants to deal with that sort of thing.

- Framers: When you're not prepared for fine framing, take it to a frame shop.

TEN STEPS TO HIRING PROFESSIONALS

Get enough information to be sure you like the work of a particular professional. Avoid one who is notoriously late or hopelessly expensive.

Pull together a visual reference of what you like from magazines and brochures. It's like picking out a hairstyle from a magazine while you're waiting for the stylist.

Make sure the professional is capable of the work you want done.

Don't ask people to come to your house without expecting to pay a consultant's fee. Go to their office (if they have one) to discuss the possibilities. Look at their portfolios of completed work.

Ask how much it will cost before any work begins.

Get a letter or contract confirming your arrangements. It should outline the work, the costs, and the payment schedule.

Nothing should be ordered until you approve it.

Once materials are ordered, don't change your mind. If you do, expect to pay for it.

Schedule the work.

The professional will begin the work and complete it as described in the contract. However, no matter what's on paper, expect to make allowances for unforeseen problems.

If You Really Want More, Read These

Publishers of books, magazines, catalogs, and Web sites expect to handle the hot trend toward simplified living that's showing itself in people polls. Everyone wants fast answers for handling life's little hassles.

EASY-STYLE DECORATING BOOKS

Here are a few quick-answer decorating books. You'll see more titles on the bookshelves in the future:

- *A Home for All Seasons* by Meg Lesser Roberts and Steven Roberts. Harry N. Abrams, Inc. New York, 1998

- *Easy Country* by Katrin Cargill. Little, Brown and Company, Boston, 1998.

- *Easy Style: 300 Decorating Shortcuts*. Better Homes and Gardens Books, Des Moines, Iowa, 1998.

- *Mary Emmerling's Quick Decorating*. Clarkson-Potter/Publishers, New York, 1997.

- *Seashore Style* by Andrea Spencer. Lorenz Books, New York, 1998.

- *The Family Home: Relaxed, Informal Living for All Ages* by Joanna Copestick. Stewart, Tabori and Chang, New York, 1998.

HOME FURNISHINGS CATALOGS

Half of getting your redecorating done is shopping for the furniture and accessories that will make it happen. These are my favorite mail-order catalogs:

- Ballard Designs, 1670 Defoor Ave. NW, Atlanta, GA 30318-7528.
- Crate and Barrel, P.O. Box 9059, Wheeling, IL 60090-9059.
- Coldwater Creek Bed & Bath, One Coldwater Creek Drive, Sandpoint, ID 83864.
- The Company Store, 500 Company Store Road, La Crosse, WI 54601.
- Cuddledown of Maine, 312 Canco Road, Portland, ME 04103.
- Linen and Lace, #4 Lafayette St., Washington, MO 63090-2541.
- Pottery Barn, Mail Order Department, P.O. Box 7044, San Francisco, CA 94120-7044.
- Restoration Hardware, 104 Challenger Drive, Portland, TN 37148-1703.
- Smith+Noble Windoware Sourcebook, 1801 California Avenue, Corona, CA 91719.

HOME ARTS MAGAZINES

Subscriptions to home and family magazines keep you aware of decorating trends and new products you can buy and use at home. Magazines are also useful for tearing out and filing away ideas in your decorating wish book. Here are a few magazines that will show you the simpler sides of decorating homes:

- *Better Homes and Gardens*, 1716 Locust St., Des Moines, IA 50309-3023.
- *Coast Living*, 2100 Lakeshore Drive, Birmingham, AL 35209.

■ *Country Home*, 1716 Locust St., Des Moines, IA 50309-3023.

■ *Martha Stewart Living*, Box 60001, Tampa, FL 33660-0001.

WEB SITES

The fledgling Internet is about to make some major hits. Here are a few Web sites worth sighting:

http://www.ballard-designs.com (Ballard Designs)

http://www.bhglive.com (*Better Homes and Gardens*)

http://www.coastallivingmag.com (*Coast Living*)

http://homearts.com (*Good Housekeeping*)

http://www.marthastewart.com (*Martha Stewart Living*)

If You Don't Know What It Means, Look Here

Decorating has a language of its own, and this book is full of terms you won't hear unless you're talking about decorating. I've done my best to inform you along the way by defining words as they're used, but here's a list you might like to review:

Amphora urn   A narrow-necked vessel with a large belly and small base once designed by the Greeks and used today as a flower vase.

Armoire   A large wardrobe or movable cupboard with doors and shelves.

Bobeche   A French word for a decorative disc at the base of a candle intended to catch dripping wax while a candle burns.

Cafe curtain   A short, informal curtain that covers the lower half of a window.

Can light   A lightbulb pointed up in the bottom of a metal can to direct light upward.

Casing   The framework around a door or window.

Ceramic tile   A floor- or wall-covering product made from clay and surfaced with a glaze for smoothness and color.

Chambray   A fine variety of gingham fabric, commonly plain in color, usually blue.

Chain-stitch   A kind of ornamental stitching in which each stitch forms a loop through the forward end of which the next stitch is taken.

Charger   A large, shallow dish under a plate to protect a tabletop from liquid spills.

Chenille   Fabric made with a fringed silken thread used as the weft in combination with wool or cotton as the wrap threads.

Chintz   A printed and glazed cotton fabric used especially for curtains.

Citronella   A fragrant Asian grass that produces oil used in making candles to repel insects.

Continental rod   A two- to three-inch-wide, flat curtain rod that slips inside a two- to three-inch-wide rod-pocketed curtain.

Craft knife   A narrow, angled, fine-tipped razor blade set into a slender handle, making a pen-sized cutting tool.

Dado   The lower, broad part of a wall covered in wallpaper, fabric, or paint.

Dhurrie   An east Indian word for a wool or cotton woven rug.

Die-cut   A process in which a steel bar is pressed through a material, such as wallpaper, to cut its shape.

Dry-mount   A dry mounting of a flexible image on a firm sheet of foam core to strengthen it.

Duvet   A quilt or plain-weave cotton comforter filled with goose down.

Duvet cover   A large envelope of fabric that slips over a duvet like a pillowcase to keep it clean.

Empire style   Interior decoration in vogue during the first French empire (1804–15).

Enamelware   Metal dishes or pots covered with an enamel surface.

Filigree   Delicate and fanciful, lacy ornamental work of scrolls and arabesques.

Finial   The ornamental cap on the end of a curtain rod.

Fluorescent light   An electric discharge lamp in which light is produced by passage of electricity through a vapor enclosed in a glass or tube.

Frieze   A decorative band on a wall.

Galvanized metal   Steel or iron covered with zinc to protect it from rust.

Grout   A thin coarse mortar poured between tiles to fill in the spaces and create a smooth surface.

Gustavian style   Swedish interior decoration during the reign of King Gustav III (1770–1810).

Head rail   The top board on a blind or shade from which it is hung.

Incandescent lamp   A lamp whose light is due to the glowing of some material, such as the common electric lamp, which contains a filament rendered luminous by the passage of current through it.

Inside mount   A curtain set inside the window frame or casing.

Ironstone   Any ore or iron with clayey or siliceous impurities used to make dishes and pottery.

Jamb   The side of an opening; a vertical piece forming the side of a doorway or window.

Laminate   To construct by placing thin layer on thin layer, as is done with wood, plastic, or paper.

Latex   A milky liquid in certain plants, such as milkweeds, poppies, or plants yielding India rubber, used to make paint or rubber rug backings.

Matchstick blind   A window covering made from slender rods of splintered wood connected by thin cording.

Mineral spirits   Turpentine; a volatile oil when distilled that will cut through the oil of paint to remove it from a brush or other surface.

Miter joint   A joint formed when two pieces of identical cross sections are joined at the ends at equal angles (as in a wood or wallpaper frame).

Muslin   A cotton fabric made in various degrees of fineness and often printed, woven, or embroidered in patterns.

Needlepoint   A mesh canvas that has been embroidered with decorative threads in a pattern or picture.

Oasis   A soft brick of floral foam used to stabilize and water plant stems set into vases.

Oil-base paint   Pigment suspended in sticky, alkyd resins that can't be cleaned up without turpentine or mineral spirits.

Outside mount   A window treatment set on the outside of a window frame or casing.

Pendant light   A lamp hung by a slender cord from the ceiling.

Pillar candle   A wide cylinder or column-like candle.

Pique   A fabric woven lengthwise with raised cords of cotton, spun rayon, or silk.

Plumb bob   A weight on a string used to measure a straight, vertical line on a wall.

Polyurethane   A finishing coat; available in both water-based and oil-based forms, polyurethane is a complex mixture of plastic resins and solvents that dries to a tough, light amber finish.

Resilient flooring   Another name for vinyl flooring due to its elastic, springing-back character.

Rya rug   A Swedish floor covering with long, shaggy threads looped through a mesh canvas backing.

Sash   A movable framework into which glass panes are set, as in a window.

Sconce   A wall bracket for holding one or more lamps or candles.

Sepia   A brownish pigment or brown tone in a picture.

Sheers   Transparently thin, diaphanous fabric used for window coverings.

Shoji screen   A Japanese movable wall made from light wood and translucent paper.

Sisal   A fiber yielded from the agave plant and made into string, ropes, and rugs.

Strip light   A narrow band of light contained by a metal casing for attaching to cabinetry.

Tabard   A loose, outer garment without sleeves; a pinafore without ties.

Tea light   Common name given to small votive candles.

Tension rod   A curtain rod that is hung by spring pressure between the sides of a window frame.

Terra cotta   A hard, usually unglazed earthenware of fine quality used for pots and vases.

Ticking   A strong, cotton fabric, usually twilled, used especially for mattress and pillow covers.

Torchere   A torch-like lamp that directs light upward.

Track light   An electrical track set on a ceiling to energize lamps that are pushed into the track.

Tung oil   A drying oil, a valuable ingredient of varnishes obtained from a Chinese tree.

Tureen   A large, deep dish with a cover.

Twill   A fabric woven with the weft threads so crossing the warp as to produce an effect of parallel diagonal lines.

Valance   A short, ornamental piece of drapery placed across the top of a window.

Velour   A French term for velvet.

Voile   A sheer, transparent, veil-like fabric.

Votive candle   A small, short cylinder of a candle that burns in a small, cylindrical container.

Wainscot   The lower portion of a wall surfaced in a different manner or material from that used for the upper portion.

Wall washer   A recessed light that can be rotated and positioned to "wash" a wall with light.

It's Time for Your Reward

Once You've Done This . . .	**Reward Yourself . . .**
Organized your decorating files and done your personal style search	Buy something significant to represent your own brand of lazy-style decorating
Assembled your toolbox of basic decorating tools	Order in a double-supreme pizza for everyone
Marked and pulled together all the decorating tools and materials you already had in the house	Go shopping for new decorating tools and toys
Taken your first decorating shortcut	Hang out in the hammock
Eased your way through a clean-up	Stand in a hot shower for a power clean-up of your own
Scaled a wall with a paintbrush and painted a signature color wall	Go for the full-body massage you've scheduled ahead of time

Once You've Done This . . .	**Reward Yourself . . .**
Laid down a lazy rug in front of the sofa	Do the couch-potato thing and enjoy the new view at your feet
Dressed a window in fresh, carefree fabrics	Take a walk in the park to breathe in the fresh air and feel as carefree as your new curtains
Created a midsummer magic hour with a new lamp	Share a chic night with a friend over a bottle of wine
Given your favorite chair a new slip	Slip into a casual cover-up of your own and relax in your chair
Rearranged the family photos in a way that really works	Sit back and riffle through old family photos still in the file
Looked in a lazy mirror you've just hung	Tell yourself what a great decorator you are
Indulged yourself with new bathroom storage	Put the kids in the tub with new bath toys
Charmed a room with a lazy flower arrangement	Light a candle, sit back, and watch the flowers unfold
Lit a candlelight dinner with your sweetheart	Share the ambience and the evening
Stretched out your living space	Take the film from your outdoor getaway to be developed

Where to Find What You're Looking For

Kitchen floors, 99
Kitchen garden, 276

Lace curtains, 128–29
Lamb's wool duster, 260
Laminate flooring,
    99–100
Latex paints, 24–25, 64,
    78–79
  three worst things to
    do with, 79
Lazy look, 14–17
  accessories, 16–17
  easy-care fabrics, 15–16
  natural colors, 14–15
  relaxed dining, 16
  sofa, 16
Lazy program, 8–10
Leaning mirrors, 189–90,
    192–93
Leaves, dried, 56
Ledges, 119
  candles on, 252–53
  displays on, 171,
    178–79
  gardens on, 291–92
Light bulbs, 146
Light control, curtains
    for, 114, 119, 121
Lighters, long-nosed,
    20–21, 46
Lighting, 135–47. See
    also Candles
  accent, 140–43
  outdoor, 282
  task, 139–40
  three worst things to
    do when buying,
    136
  types of, 136–39
Linen and Lace, 304
Long-nosed lighters,
    20–21, 46

Low bowler, 235–36
Luminaria, 247

Magazines, 304–5
Magnetic rods, 27, 28
Magnetic tapes, 30
Magnifying mirrors, 190
Mail-order catalogs, 13,
    17, 191, 304
Marble floors, 100–101
Marbles, 31–32, 226
Martha Stewart Living,
    305
Matchstick blinds, 122
Materials, 19, 23–32.
    See also specific
    materials
Measuring tape, 20, 22,
    116, 155
  miniature, 42, 116
Milk carriers, 227,
    234–35
Miniature lights, 142–43.
    See also Christmas
    tree lights
Mirrors, 58, 187–201
  advantages of using,
    188–89
  arrangements of, 193,
    194–96
  candles and, 254
  cleaning, 194
  hanging, 190, 192,
    197–200
  incorporating into
    scheme, 192–93
  parts of, 188
  size and style of,
    189–90
  where to buy, 191–92
Miter joints, 93–94
Mopping, 69
Mouse sanders, 23, 162

Music, decorating, 47
My Sister Shabby style,
    13

Nail hole filler, 24–25, 46
Natural colors, 14–15
Natural floor coverings,
    101, 105–6
Natural light, 143–44
Non-directional wall-
    paper borders,
    89–90, 92, 93
Non-splatter wall-
    painting tools, 25,
    64, 78, 81

Oasis, 31
Office
  in a box, 211–12
  inventory of, 205–6
Oil-based paints, 64
Oil lamps, 45
Oil soap, 69
One-color accent band,
    85
Organization. See
    Decorating closet;
    Storage
Oriental weave rugs,
    104
Outdoor decorating tips,
    276–82
Outdoor furniture,
    278–80
Oversize mirrors,
    189–90, 192–93

Paintbrushes, 24–25, 40
  clean-up tips, 64–65
Painters, professional,
    300
Painter's tape, 24–25, 84
Painter's tray, 24–25

Seam repair adhesive, 26, 46, 94
Seat cushions, 151, 154, 158–59
Sensibility, personal, 4, 11–13. *See also* Style search
Serving carts, 214–15
Settee, 209
Shades, 27–28, 115, 119, 122–24, 145
  hanging, 122–24
  opaque, 138, 144
  three worst things to do when shopping for, 122
Shears. *See* Scissors
Sheer curtains, 119, 126–29
Shelves, 212–13
Sherwin Williams, 25–26
Side tables, 165–66
Signature color, 6–7, 44
Simply Chic style, 13
Sisal rugs, 101, 105
Six-by-eight-foot rugs, 107
Slate floors, 100–1
Slipcovers, 153–59
  loose, 154–56
  semi-fitted, 157
  tight fit, 156–57
Slotted screwdrivers, 21
Small curtains, 130–31
Smith + Noble Windoware Sourcebook, 304
Snapshot gallery, 172–76
Sofas
  hanging picture above, 183
  for outdoors, 278–79

slipcovering, 153–57
style of, 16
Speed painting, 80–88
Spilled wax, 72–73, 247
Spills, 70
Sponges, cellulose, 20–21, 41
Spot lifter, 29–30, 46
Spray painting, 64, 161
Spring cleaning, 50–51
Spring decorating tips, 50–53
Stain markers, wood-finish, 29–30, 46
Stains, 70
  removing, 151–52
  three worst things to do when facing, 150
Staple gun and staples, 23
Starter sets, tool, 22
Storage, 203–19. *See also* Decorating closet
  bath, 213–14
  closets, 208–9
  clutter-busting, 207–8
  cupboards, 208–10
  hassle-free, 215–16
  office in a box, 211–12
  three worst ways to choose, 217
  three worst ways to handle, 213
Storage pieces, 208
Strip lights, 136, 139–40
Stud sensors, 20, 22
Style files, 7–9, 12, 44
Style names, 11–13
Style search, 4, 11–13
  decorating diary and, 7–9, 12, 44

for personal color, 5–7, 44
style names, 11–13
Styling kit, 42–43
Styling tricks, 259–74
Suitcases, 209
Summer decorating tips, 53–55
Sunlight, 143–44
Sunscreen, 281
Supplies. *See* Materials
Swedish Romantic style, 13
Sweeping up, 67
Synagogue candles, 45, 244

Table lamps, 136, 137–38, 144–45
Tables, outdoors, 280
Table settings, 262–68
Tabletop displays, 171, 177–78
Tab-top curtains, 27, 120, 129–30
Tack cloth, 29, 46
Tape measure, 20, 22, 116, 155
  miniature, 42, 116
Tapers, 45, 243
Task lighting, 139–40
Tea lights, 45, 244
Tension rods, 27–28, 46, 132–33
Terrace, 276–77
Tile layers, 300
Tool belts, 43
Toolbox, 20, 39–40
Tools, 19–33. *See also* *specific tools*
  basic, 20–22
  buying tips, 21–23

Now you can do these tasks, too!

The Lazy Way

Starting to think there are a few more of life's little tasks that you've been putting off? Don't worry—we've got you covered. Take a look at all of *The Lazy Way* books available. Just imagine—you can do almost anything *The Lazy Way!*

Handle Your Money The Lazy Way
By Sarah Young Fisher and Carol Turkington
0-02-862632-X

Build Your Financial Future The Lazy Way
By Terry Meany
0-02-862648-6

Cut Your Spending The Lazy Way
By Leslie Haggin
0-02-863002-5

Have Fun with Your Kids The Lazy Way
By Marilee Lebon
0-02-863166-8

Keep Your Kids Busy The Lazy Way
By Barbara Nielsen and Patrick Wallace
0-02-863013-0

Feed Your Kids Right The Lazy Way
By Virginia Van Vynckt
0-02-863001-7

*All Lazy Way books are just $12.95!

additional titles on the back!

Learn French The Lazy Way
By Christophe Desmaison
0-02-863011-4

Learn German The Lazy Way
By Amy Kardel
0-02-863165-X

Learn Italian The Lazy Way
By Gabrielle Euvino
0-02-863014-9

Learn Spanish The Lazy Way
By Steven Hawson
0-02-862650-8

Shed Some Pounds The Lazy Way
By Annette Cain and Becky Cortopassi-Carlson
0-02-862999-X

Shop Online The Lazy Way
By Richard Seltzer
0-02-863173-0

Clean Your House The Lazy Way
By Barbara H. Durham
0-02-862649-4

Care for Your Home The Lazy Way
By Terry Meany
0-02-862646-X

Stop Aging The Lazy Way
By Judy Myers, Ph.D.
0-02-862793-8

Get in Shape The Lazy Way
By Annette Cain
0-02-863010-6

Learn to Sew The Lazy Way
By Lydia Wills
0-02-863167-6

Train Your Dog The Lazy Way
By Andrea Arden
0-87605180-8

Organize Your Stuff The Lazy Way
By Toni Ahlgren
0-02-863000-9

Manage Your Time The Lazy Way
By Toni Ahlgren
0-02-863169-2

Take Care of Your Car The Lazy Way
By Michael Kennedy and Carol Turkington
0-02-862647-8

Get a Better Job The Lazy Way
By Susan Ireland
0-02-863399-7

Cook Your Meals The Lazy Way
By Sharon Bowers
0-02-862644-3

Cooking Vegetarian The Lazy Way
By Barbara Grunes
0-02-863158-7

Master the Grill The Lazy Way
By Pamela Rice Hahn and Keith Giddeon
0-02-863157-9